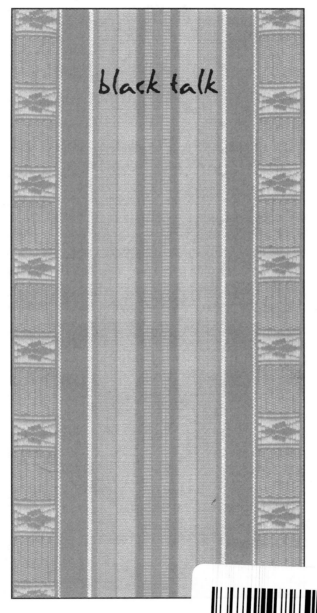

black talk

ALSO BY
GENEVA SMITHERMAN

BLACK LANGUAGE AND CULTURE:
SOUNDS OF SOUL

THE VOICE OF BLACK AMERICA
(SET OF 12 CASSETTE TAPES)

TALKIN AND TESTIFYIN:
THE LANGUAGE OF BLACK AMERICA

BLACK ENGLISH AND THE EDUCATION
OF BLACK CHILDREN AND YOUTH

DISCOURSE AND DISCRIMINATION

AND AIN'T I A WOMAN?:
AFRICAN AMERICAN WOMEN
AND AFFIRMATIVE ACTION

ANITA HILL — CLARENCE THOMAS:
RACE, CLASS, AND GENDER

BLACK TALK

Words and Phrases
from the Hood to
the Amen Corner

GENEVA
SMITHERMAN

HOUGHTON MIFFLIN COMPANY

BOSTON   NEW YORK   1994

For information about permission to reproduce selections
from this book, write to Permissions, Houghton Mifflin Company,
215 Park Avenue South, New York, New York 10003.

Library of Congress Cataloging-in-Publication Data

Smitherman, Geneva, date.
Black talk: words and phrases from the hood to the amen corner/
Geneva Smitherman.
p.   cm.
Includes bibliographical references (p.).
ISBN 0-395-67410-7 (cl)   ISBN 0-395-69992-4 (pa)
1. English language—United States—Glossaries, vocabularies, etc.
2. English language—United States—Slang—Dictionaries.
3. Afro-Americans—Language—Dictionaries.
4. Black English—Dictionaries.
5. Americanisms—Dictionaries.   1. Title.
PE3102.N4S65   1994
427'.973'08996—dc20   94-591
CIP

Book design by Anne Chalmers

Printed in the United States of America

BP 10 9 8 7 6 5 4 3 2 1

Permissions appear on page 244

FOR MY SON, TONY,
AND HIS CHILDREN,
ANTHONY AND AMBER,
AND FUTURE GENERATIONS
ALL OVER THIS LAND

ACKNOWLEDGMENTS

This project was started back in the 1970s when my editor at the time asked me to prepare a small glossary of terms and expressions for inclusion in *Talkin and Testifyin: The Language of Black America,* which was subsequently published by Houghton Mifflin in 1977. In the years since then, I have been gradually adding to that initial collection, and numerous people have helped to bring this project to fruition at last. Of course, any mistakes or shortcomings in this book are entirely my own.

First, a word of gratitude for language research in the hood done by hundreds of students in my courses over the years at Harvard University, Wayne State University, and Michigan State University.

For responding to my call for language surveys and sound advice, I am indebted to: Ana Celia Zentella, Yusuf Nuruddin, and Milton Baxter of New York City; Sandra Wright of New Orleans; Deputy Police Chief Benny Napoleon of Detroit; Gregory Moore of Chicago and Abdul Alkalimat of Chicago and Boston; Mashana (Deucette) and Milbrun (Deuce) Pearson, Sterling Beasley, Nicole Smith, and Kenny Snodgrass of Detroit; Gary Simpkins and Edward Boyer of Los Angeles; Nathan Magee of Stockton and the Bay Area in California; James Ward of Houston; Perry Hall of Chapel Hill, North Carolina, and Ronn Hopkins of Bath, North Carolina; Christianna Buchner of Munich, Germany; Ron Stephens of Philadelphia and Detroit.

For helpful word lists, I thank John Rickford of Stanford, California; Hilton Morris of Fort Wayne, Indiana; Ronald Butters of Durham, North Carolina; Police Chief Robert L. Johnson of Jackson, Michigan.

For steering me to legendary sources of language in the hood, I thank Henry (White Cap) Rupert and all of his Old School gangsta partners, but especially Lyin Willie of Chicago, Diamond Joe of Atlanta, Old Mose and Slick Trick of Los Angeles, Hustlin Arthur of Detroit, Slim Jim of Dallas, and the Bad Dudes of East St. Louis and Yazoo, Mississippi.

A shout out to Milbrun (Deuce) Pearson for pulling me aside back in 1989 and making me give a serious listen to Rap Music. And to Kofi Davis and Kwame Finn for introducing me to Underground Rap and serving as guides to the oral culture of Hip Hop. Thanks, Youngbloods.

My student research assistants, Kerry Rockquemore and Nicole Smith, deserve special recognition. In addition to processing data cards, typing and retyping and retyping, they assisted in the tedious process of tracking down permission rights and aided me in the thousand and one laborious and painstaking details necessary to complete this kind of dictionary. Thanks to Nicole for going above and beyond the call of duty in countless ways. Much appreciation to Kerry for being a diligent researcher and a stickler for details—and for tolerating my phone calls late in the midnight hour.

A project of this sort needs the guiding hand of a wise and understanding editor. Fortunately, I had such an editor in the person of Elizabeth (Liz) Kubik. I have benefited immeasurably from her advice and experience. Many thanks, Girlfriend.

In writer and scholar Dr. Keith Gilyard I found a kindred spirit with a profound understanding of the cultural significance of and critical necessity for this book. Keith read and reread and reread—eventually, we lost count—the entire manuscript.

Each time his sharp intellect and poetic vision—and his mother wit—brought forth new insights for me to ponder. He is testimony to the intellectual-activist's commitment to the Black Tradition and to the people who create and nurture that Tradition. We owe you, my brotha.

Not least of all, I owe a debt of gratitude to the millions of African Americans who talk that Talk in the churches, at senior-citizen bingo games, in daylong hair-braiding gatherings of women, at family reunions, on the buses and subways, playing pickup basketball, in bars and comedy clubs, at house parties, dances and concerts, at community meetings and political rallies—and wherever Black people congregate. Actually, this entire country is indebted to Africans in America for enriching and enlivening Americans' daily conversation with words and phrases from the hood to the Amen Corner.

Geneva Smitherman

January 1994

CONTENTS

Hey, DOG, WHASS HAPNIN?
Middle-aged lawyer
greeting an old fraternity buddy

I don't have no time for no "WHAM BAM, THANK
    YOU, MAM!"
Gas me up, git me drunk, and HIT THE SKINS and
    scram.
Singer/Rapper Mary J. Blige,
from her 1992 album What's the 411?

When they tell you yo cancer in remission, all that mean
is that bad boy LAYIN IN THE CUT waitin for YO ass!
Middle-aged female nurse

I own know what dem white folk talkin bout—we never
did git our FORTY ACRES!
Senior female, retired domestic worker

What RED, BLACK AND GREEN AFRIKAN B-BOY
wouldn't want to go over to this twentysomething,
Brooklyn FLYgirl's CRIB?
Louis Romain, "A Rose Grows in Brooklyn,"
in The Source, *July, 1993*

The Spirit got holt to him, he went to hollin and moanin
and goin on, next thang I know he TALKIN IN
TONGUE!
Senior male, church deacon,
retired blue-collar worker

Crack or SMACK-uh take you to a sho end
You don't need it, jes throw that stuff away
You wanna git HIGH, let the record play.
Rapper Ice-T, from his 1988 Power *album*

INTRODUCTION

❖ ❖ ❖ ❖ ❖ ❖ ❖ ❖

Word from the
African American Community

Everyday people, African Americans from all walks of life ... "talkin and TESTIFYin"...LYIN and SIGNIFYIN... WORKin IT. This dictionary captures just a slice of the dynamic, colorful span of language in the African American community. (This language will be referred to as Black Talk, African American English, AAE, Black/African American Language, Ebonics, and Black/African American lingo.) You will find words and expressions in current use by all segments of the community—seniors and B-BOYS, FLYGUYS and LAMES, FIVE PERCENTERS and the AMEN CORNER, reverends and ROLLERS, the AFRICAN-CENTERED and WANNABES. From the JUMP, understand that when it comes to Black Talk, the "boyz in the HOOD" do not have a corner on the market. Sure, HIP HOP has given us DEF and DOPE rhymes, but senior AFRICAN women had us dying laughing when we PEEPed what membership in the PACKER'S CLUB means. Through the "Def Comedy Jam" Movement, we made the acquaintance of BÉ-BÉ'S KIDS, and the CRIPS and BLOODS have taught us more than we ever wanted to know about AKS and NINES. But the 1960s Black Freedom Struggle[1] is the source of today's X caps, and ALLEY BALL players from the OLD SCHOOL established the tradition of SHOOTing THE DIE. (By the way, if any of the aforementioned lost you, the dictionary gives the meanings of all the words in this introduction shown in small capital letters.)

Black Talk crosses boundaries—of sex, age, region, religion, social class—because the language comes from the same source: the African American Experience and the Oral Tradition[2] embedded in that Experience. On one level, there is great diversity among African Americans today, but on a deeper level, race continues to be the defining core of the Black Experience. While today's Hip Hop Culture is contributing its own special lingo unrelated to race—phrases such as ALL THAT, IN THE MIX, GIT WIT—it is also reintroducing race-conscious language from previous generations. For example, filmmaker Spike Lee named his production company "FORTY ACRES AND A MULE," a Black expression that goes all the way back to the nineteenth century. His parents' and grandparents' generations put the goal of land for the "Black Nation" on the COMMUNITY's agenda. In the early years of this century, this idea was put forth by various Black Nationalist intellectuals, notably Marcus Garvey. In the 1960s, the concept was worked out in detailed clarity by the Republic of New Africa, embodied in its call for "five states"[3] as reparations for Blacks. Both *forty acres* and "five states" take us back to the post–Civil War era and the bill passed by Congress in 1866. This legislation was designed to strengthen the Freedmen's Bureau (the Federal agency set up to resettle ex-slaves). The most interesting part of the bill, and the most controversial, stipulated that each household of ex-slaves would receive an allotment of forty acres of land (plus some start-up resources, captured in the expression that has come down to us, *forty acres, fifty dollars, and a mule*). This payment for 246 years of free African labor not only would have provided reparations for enslavement but also would have established a base for self-sufficiency and initiated the economic development of the African American community. President Andrew Johnson, taking over after President Abraham Lincoln's assassination, vetoed the bill, and Congress was either unable, or unwilling, to override the veto. The nation's 1866 failure to right the wrong of enslavement continues to haunt Blacks, particularly in this period of severe economic crises and of devastating social effects that result from an underdeveloped community.

A similar example exists in the concept of COOL, although at first glance this might not seem to be a race-conscious idea. However, a disempowered group daily forced to face the possibility of its destruction can ill afford to be HOT. With lynch mobs in the old days, police brutality in this new day—any heat generated by rage and anger could literally be dangerous to a Black person's health. Hence the value of calmness and maintaining your *cool* as a survival strategy. Today's African American youth talk about CHILLIN, their middle-aged parents still call it being *cool,* and an eighty-five-year-old Black man recently referred to the cool coping style as COPASETIC.

This dictionary takes you beyond a word list. It is a cultural map that charts word meanings along the highways and byways of African American life. In order to understand idioms like EUROPEAN NEGRO, ARE YOU RIGHT?, and HIGH YELLUH and words like HOODOO, BAD, and HONKY, you need to understand how and why this nation within a nation developed its unique way of using the English language. Which brings us to history and the importance of the past in understanding—and moving beyond—the present.

"WHAT IS AFRICA TO ME?"

> What is Africa to me
> Copper sun or scarlet sea,
> Jungle star or jungle track,
> Strong bronzed men, or regal black,
> Women from whose loins I sprang

> When the birds of Eden sang?
> One three centuries removed
> From the scenes his fathers loved,
> Spicy grove, cinnamon tree,
> What is Africa to me?
>
> —Countee Cullen, "Heritage" (1925)

Down through the years, and especially in the decades since the Civil War, generations of African Americans have asked themselves the question posed by Harlem Renaissance[4] writer Countee Cullen. Long since removed from their native land, many Black Americans feel the same as some Blacks in a 1989 opinion poll I conducted on the name change from "BLACK" to "AFRICAN AMERICAN": "We are more American than African; we have been here too long," and "What do they mean about African American? By now we have no African in us." On the other hand, there are also many Black Americans who acknowledge a connection to Africa, what one of the people in the opinion poll called "our origin and cultural identity."

As far as historians, linguists, and other scholars go, during the first half of this century it was widely believed that enslavement had wiped out all traces of African languages and cultures, and that Black "differences" resulted from imperfect and inadequate imitations of EUROPEAN AMERICAN language and culture. George Philip Krapp, writing in the 1920s, is one linguist who held this view about the speech of Africans in America. In the 1960s these opinions came under close scrutiny and were soundly challenged by a number of experts, such as the historian John Blassingame and the linguist J. L. Dillard. Today scholars generally agree that the African heritage was not totally wiped out, and that both African American Language and African American Culture have roots in African patterns. (This view had also been advanced by anthropologist Melville Herskovits and linguist Lorenzo Dow Turner in the 1930s and 1940s, but they were a distinct minority in those days.) Over time, and after prolonged contact with European Americans, Africans in America adopted some Eurocentric patterns, and their African patterns of language and culture were modified—but they were not erased. African American Language and Culture, then, reflects a dual heritage. As Dr. W. E. B. DuBois put it nearly a century ago in *Souls of Black Folk,* "One ever feels his two-ness—an American, a Negro."

The uniqueness of AAE is evident in three areas: (1) patterns of grammar and pronunciation, many of which reflect the patterns that operate in West African languages (for example, many West African languages don't have the English "th" sounds, and in AAE "th" is rendered with the next closest sound, as a "d," a "t," or an "f"); (2) verbal rituals from the Oral Tradition and the continued importance of the Word, as in African cultures; and (3) lexicon, or vocabulary, usually developed by giving special meanings to regular English words, a practice that goes back to enslavement and the need for a system of communication that only those in the enslaved community could understand.

Although here we are concerned only with the words that make up the lexicon, there are correct ways of saying these words, of talking Black, that is, that depend on knowledge of the rules of AAE grammar and pronunciation. Like the popular DJ said to a DUDE who phoned in a request for D. J. Jazzy Jeff & The Fresh Prince's JAM "Summertime": "Okay, man, I'll play it for you, but see, it ain't summer*time*, it's summa*h*time."

A complete inventory and analysis of AAE grammar and pronunciation and its African language sources is beyond the scope of this introduction. This Africanized style of speaking the English language is a complicated system, made even more complex by the existence of Euro-American patterns of English within the Africanized English system. Interested readers may consult Lorenzo Dow Turner's *Africanisms in the Gullah Dialect;* Molefi Kete Asante's "African Elements in African American English" in Joseph Holloway's excellent collection, *Africanisms in American Culture;* J. L. Dillard's *Black English;* Mervyn Alleyne's *Comparative Afro-American;* my own *Talkin and Testifyin;* John Baugh's *Black Street Speech;* Walter Wolfram and Nona H. Clarke's *Black-White Speech Relationships;* Hanni U. Taylor's *Standard English, Black English, and Bidialectalism;* and William Labov's *Language in the Inner City.*

Listed below are only a few of the patterns of AAE grammar and pronunciation; these patterns are found in some of the words and expressions in this dictionary:

1. *Final and post-vocalic "r."* The "r" sound at the end of a word and after a vowel is not heard in AAE. Instead, use a vowel sound, as in "summ*ah*time," as that big-city DJ instructed his caller. The expression "Sure, you're right" becomes SHOW YOU RIGHT. "Torn up" would be TOE UP. Use YO instead of "your." And RAP Music's popular, if controversial, word HO is the AAE pronunciation of "whore." (Not to be confused with "hoe," as the white teacher in the film *House Party* did when she asked her Black male student why he called another Black male student's mother a "garden tool.")

2. *Final and medial consonants.* Reduce to a vowel sound, or a single consonant sound. Thus, for example, "cold" is COAL in AAE. This can get a bit complicated if a word requires the operation of two rules simultaneously, as for example in the phrase "torn up," where the double consonant "rn" must be reduced, and at the same time, the "r" after the vowel sound deleted. Applying the rules correctly gives you *toe*, not "ton," as a beginning student of Black lingo produced.

3. *Stress on the first syllable.* For most words, put the stress, or emphasis, on the first syllable of the word. For example, AAE speakers say PO-leece, not po-LEECE, and DE-troit, not De-TROIT.

4. *The vowel sound in words that rhyme with "think" and "ring."* In AAE, this vowel is pronounced like the vowel in "thank" and "rang." Thus, "sing" is rendered as *sang*, "drink" is pronounced *drank,* etc. This pattern produced the *thang* of Dr. Dre's "Nuthin' But a 'G' Thang," from his 1992 album *The Chronic.*

5. *Indicate tense (time) by context, not with an "s" or "ed."* For example, "Mary do anythang she want to" and "They look for him everywhere but never did find him."

6. *"Be" and "Bees" to indicate continuous action or infrequently recurring activity.* For example, "Every time we see him, he be dressed like that." This is the rule that produced "It bees dat way," which may be shortened to simply BEES.

7. *Final "th" sounds become "t" or "f."* This pattern gives us DEF, as in "Def Comedy Jam," from the 1970s expression *doin it to death,* with the final "th" in "death" pronounced as an "f." This is also where WIT, as in the HIP HOP phrase GIT WIT *you,* comes from, with the final "th" in "with" rendered as a "t" sound.

8. *Is* and *Are* in sentences. These words aren't necessary to make full statements; nor are the contracted forms of these words (that is, the "'s" for "is" and the "'re" for "are"). This is the rule that allows *What up?* for "What's up?"

The African American Oral Tradition is rooted in a belief in the power of the Word. The African concept of *Nommo*, the Word, is believed to be the force of life itself. To speak is to make something come into being; thus senior Black Americans will often use the cautionary statement "Don't speak on it" in the face of some negative possibility GOin DOWN. On the other hand, once something is given the force of speech, it is binding—hence the familiar saying "Yo word is yo bond," which in today's Hip Hop Culture has become WORD IS BORN. The Hip Hop expressions WORD, WORD UP, WORD TO THE MOTHER, and similar phrases all stem from the value placed on speech. Creative, highly verbal talkers are valued; RAPPin, LYIN, SIGNIFYIN, TESTIFYin, PLAYin THE DOZENS, WOOFin—skillful use of these and other verbal rituals from the Oral Tradition is what gets a person PROPS. Which is not at all to say that African Americans DIS the written word. However, like other groups with a surviving Oral Tradition, such as Native Americans, "book learning" and written documents are believed to be limited in what they can convey and teach. CHECK OUT the EDUCATED FOOL.

While it may be an A AND B CONVERSATION, Black Talk requires dialogue between "A" and "B," not "A" lecturing to "B." The idea is that constant exchange is necessary for real communication to take place. Scholars refer to this style of talk as "Call-Response." It has been ritualized in the Traditional Black Church,[5] particularly in the back-and-forth exchange between the preacher and the congregation during the sermon. But even outside the Church, whenever African Americans CONVERSATE, Call-Response abounds. Often the verbal responses are punctuated by different kinds of FIVES. The only wrong thing you can do in a Black conversation is not respond at all, because it suggests that you ain WIT the conversation. BET and WORD are Hip Hop responses that affirm what is being said, as does the older expression, SHOW YOU RIGHT. SCARED OF YOU is a response that acknowledges and celebrates some special achievement or unique action or statement, while SHUT THE NOISE!, as well as the older variation, SHUT UP!, means the exact opposite of what it says, that is, "Keep up the noise, Talk on, I'm wit that!"

The Black Church has been the single most significant force in nurturing the surviving African language and cultural traditions of African America. Over the centuries, the Church has stood as a rich reservoir of terms and expressions in Black lingo. Straight outa the Church have come expressions like ON TIME, to acknowledge that something occurred at the appropriate psychological moment, and BROTHA/SISTA, as generic terms for any African American; proverbs such as GOD DON'T LIKE UGLY and WHAT GO ROUND COME ROUND; and the ritual of SHOUTin and GITtin THE SPIRIT when moved by the musical "spirit" at SOUL concerts, clubs, cabarets, and other places of entertainment. In the spirit-getting, tongue-speaking, vision-receiving, Amen-saying, sing-song preaching, holy-dancing Traditional Black Church, the Oral Tradition is LIVE! This is so because the Church has not been pressured to take on Eurocentric culture and speech. As the only independent African American institution, the Black Church does not have to answer to white[6] folk!

Paramount in the African American Experience, the Church is a religious as well as a social unit in the community. True enough, the Church adopted Euro-American Christianity, but it Africanized this Christianity. The Church maintained the African concept of the unity of the sacred and secular worlds. That is, all of life is viewed as holy. No wonder, then, that many popular singers came out of the Church and comfortably shift back and forth between the Church and the "world"—DIVA Aretha Franklin comes immediately to mind. Such entertainers incorporate elements of the communication style of the Church into their musical style—James Brown is an excellent example. Today's Hip Hop groups borrow richly from James Brown, which is to say that they are actually reflecting the Africanized communication style of the Church through this borrowing.

What is Africa to the lingo of today's HOODS? It is the source of Nommo and the BLOOD's respect for and celebration of the power of the Word, as can be witnessed today in Rap. It made possible the development of the African American Oral Tradition. It provided the basis for the integrity of Black grammar and the Black Lexicon. Africa is the MOTHERSHIP. And while not all of African American Language and Culture can be traced to African language patterns, a lot of it can. As an ex-enslaved African once said, "Everythang I tells you am the truth, but they's plenty I can't tell you."

FROM AFRICAN TO AFRICAN AMERICAN

Just as we were called colored, but were not that . . . and then Negro, but not that . . . to be called Black is just as baseless. . . . Black tells you about skin color and what side of town you live on. African American evokes discussion of the world.

— Reverend Jesse Jackson, quoted in Clarence Page, "African American or Black? It's Debatable," in the *Detroit Free Press*, January 1, 1989, and in Isabel Wilkerson, "Many Who Favor Black Favor New Term for Who They Are," in the *New York Times*, January 31, 1989.

Names for the race have been a continuing issue since GIDDYUP, 1619, when the first slave ship landed at Jamestown. From "AFRICAN" to "COLORED" to "negro" to "NEGRO" (with the capital) to "BLACK" to "AFRICAN AMERICAN," with side trips to "AFROAMERICAN," "AFRIAMERICAN," "AFRAAMERICAN," and "AFRIKAN" — what are we Africans in America, today thirty-five million strong, "we people who are darker than blue," as Curtis Mayfield once sang, to call ourselves?

Debates rage. The topic is discussed at conferences. Among leaders and intellectuals, as well as among everyday people, the issue is sometimes argued so hotly that folk stop speaking to each other! In 1904, the *A.M.E. Church Review* sponsored a symposium of Black leaders to debate whether the "n" of "negro" should be capitalized. However, participants at that symposium went beyond the mere question of capitalization to debate whether "negro" was the right name for the race in the first place. In 1967, during the shift from "Negro" to "Black," and again in 1989, during the shift from "Black" to "African American," *Ebony* magazine devoted several pages to the question "What's in a Name?" And the beat goes on . . . because the status of Blacks remains unsettled. Name changes and debates over names reflect our uncertain status and come to the forefront during crises and upheavals in the Black condition.

Although African Americans are linked to Africans on the Continent and in the DIASPORA, the Black American, as the late writer James Baldwin once put it, is a unique creation. For one thing, other Diasporic Africans claim citizenship in countries that are virtually all Black—Jamaicans, Bajans, Nigerians, Ghanaians, etc., are not minorities in their native lands. For another, not only are Blacks a distinct minority in America, but our status as first-class citizens is debatable, even at this late hour in U.S. history. As the SISTA said about Rodney King's beating in Los Angeles, the torching of a Black man by whites in Florida, and Malice Green's death in Detroit, "After all we done been through, here it is 1992, and we still ain free." Some activists and AFRICAN-CENTERED Blacks have coined the term NEO-SLAVERY to capture the view that the present Black condition, with whites still powerful and Blacks still powerless, is just enslavement in another form.

Blacks are a minority amidst a population who look distinctly different physically and who promote race supremacist standards of physical attractiveness. This state of affairs has created a set of negative attitudes about skin color, hair, and other physical features that are reflected in the Black Lexicon—terms such as GOOD HAIR, BAD HAIR, HIGH YELLUH, LIVER-LIPS. Because black skin color was so devalued at one time, to call an African person "black" was to CALL him or her OUTA THEY NAME. It was: "If you white, you all right, if you brown, stick around, if you Black, git back." Thus the necessity, during the Black Freedom Struggle of the 1960s and 1970s, of purging the racial label "Black" and adopting it as a name for the race in symbolic celebration of the changed status of Africans in America.

Back to the RIP. The British colonists, who would become Americans in 1776, called the Africans "free" (a few were, but most were not), "slave," or, following fifteenth century Portuguese slave traders, *negro* (a Portuguese adjective, meaning "black"). [*Negro* is also a Spanish adjective that means "black"; however, the Portuguese were the first to use the term in reference to Africans.] But the Africans called themselves "African" and so designated their churches and organizations—as in the names "African Educational and Benevolent Society," "African Episcopal Church," and "African Masonic Lodge No. 459." In those early years, the thought was Africa on my mind and in my MIND'S EYE. Enslaved Africans kept thinking and hoping, all the way up until the nineteenth century, that they would one day return to Mother Africa. Some hummed the tune "I'll Fly Away," believing that, like the legendary hero Solomon, they would be able to fly back to Africa. And especially after fighting at Lexington, Concord, and Bunker Hill in America's Revolutionary War, they just knew they would be free to return home. Instead, the thirteen British colonies that became the United States tightened the reins on their African slaves, passing laws abolishing temporary enslavement and indentured servitude for Africans and making them slaves for life.

By 1800, several generations of Africans had been born on American soil, thousands had been transported from Africa, and the Black population numbered over one million. Both the vision and the possibility of returning to Africa had become impractical and remote. Further, a movement had begun to abolish slavery and to make the Africans citizens. And both free and enslaved Africans were becoming critically aware of their contributions to the development of American wealth. In light of this new reality and in preparation for citizenship and what they thought would be opportunities to enjoy the national wealth they had helped create through two hundred years of free labor, enslaved Africans began to call themselves "Colored" (often spelled "coloured" in those days), and the designation "African" declined in use.

"Colored" was used throughout much of the nineteenth century, until the white backlash began. The year 1877 marked the end of Reconstruction and set the stage for "the Coloreds" to be put back in their "place." The political deal cut in D.C.[7] led to the withdrawal of the Federal/Union troops that had been stationed in the South to ensure justice for the ex-enslaved Africans. Power and home rule were returned to the Old Confederacy. The "freedmen" (as they were called by the Federal Government and whites) lost the small gains in education, citizenship, and political power that the Civil War and the Emancipation Proclamation had made possible. New forms of repression and torture began—lynch mobs, the Ku Klux Klan, the loss of voting rights, and the beginning of separate but (UN)equal. By 1900, the quest was on for a new name to capture the new reality of being neither "slave nor free," as one ex-enslaved African put it.

Although some Colored had begun using and rallying for the label "negro," when the National Association for the Advancement of Colored People (NAACP) was founded in 1909, the COMMUNITY had not yet reached group consensus. The push for "negro" and for its capitalization hit its full stride during the period between the two World Wars. The vision was that with the U.S. campaign to "make the world safe for democracy," and with Colored soldiers shedding their blood for America, surely the yet-unsettled contradictory status of Africans in America would be resolved on the side of first-class citizenship and economic equity. Leaders such as Dr. W. E. B. DuBois, editor of the NAACP journal, *Crisis,* launched a massive nationwide effort to capitalize "negro" and to elevate the Portuguese-derived adjective "negro" to a level of dignity and respect. The NAACP mailed out over seven hundred letters to publishers and editors. Community newsletters addressed the issue, debates were held, and the name issue was addressed in talks and sermons in the Traditional Black Church. By 1930, the major European American media were using "Negro" and capitalizing it. (The two glaring exceptions were *Forum* magazine and the U.S. Government Printing Office.) The *New York Times* put it this way: "[This] is not merely a typographical change, it is an act in recognition of racial self-respect for those who have been for generations in the 'lower case'."

"Negro" was the name until the 1960s, when Africans in America struggled to throw off the shackles of Jim Crow and embraced Black Culture, the Black Experience—and black skin color. Again, conferences were held, many under the rubric of "Black Power," debates ensued, and yes, folk had hot arguments and FELL OUT with one another about abandoning the name "Negro" for "Black," which was "only an adjective." However, the motion of history could not be stopped. The name change to "Black" and the profound significance of this change in the language and life of Blacks was captured in a 1968 hit song by James Brown: "Say it Loud (I'm Black, and I'm Proud)."

The final period in the name debate (for now at least) began in late 1988 with a proposal from Dr. Ramona Edelin, president of the National Urban Coalition, to call the upcoming 1989 summit the "African American," rather than the "Black," Summit. She asserted that this name change "would establish a cultural context for the new agenda." Her view was that present-day Africans in America were facing a new reality—the erosion of hard-won progress since the late 1970s, high unemployment, the rise of racism, the growth of urban youth violence, the proliferation of crack and other drugs, and the general deterioration of the community. The situation called for reassessment within the framework of a global identity linking Africans in North America with those on the Continent and throughout the Diaspora.

As in previous eras, the name issue, this time around being the shift from "Black" to "African American," has been debated at community forums and conferences. It has been the topic of conversation and heated arguments at the barber shop and the BEAUTY SHOP, at family reunions, social gatherings, and at Church events. The change has not been as cataclysmic, though, as the shift from "Negro" to "Black" was in the 1960s, since "African American" lacks the negative history of "Black." Further, "African American" returns us to the source—the "African" of early years, but with a significant dimension added: "American." This addition calls attention to four hundred years of building wealth in America and legitimates the demand for political and economic equity. This is what David Walker, one of the first RED, BLACK, AND GREEN DUDES, conveyed in his *Appeal, in four Articles: Together with a Preamble to the Coloured Citizens of the World, but in particular, and very Expressly, to those of the United States of America.* His *Appeal* was published in 1829 during the era of "Colored." Calling for open rebellion against enslavement, and opposing the American Colonization Society's plan to resettle enslaved Africans in parts of Africa, Walker wrote:

> Men who are resolved to keep us in eternal wretchedness are also bent on sending us to Liberia. . . . America is more our

country than it is the whites—we have enriched it with our BLOOD AND TEARS.

To date, "African American" appears to have caught on throughout the community, although "Black" continues to be used also (and to a lesser extent, the name "African"/ "Afrikan"). In opinion polls about the name issue, Black youth are the strongest supporters of "African American," which is not surprising, given the African-Centered consciousness emerging in HIP HOP Culture. However, there are those—generally the parents and older siblings of the youth—who still favor "Black" because this name generated an intense, long-overdue struggle over old, past scripts of racial self-hatred and because the eventual adoption of the name "Black" symbolized a victorious shift to the positive in the African American psyche.

"THEY DONE TAKEN MY BLUES AND GONE": BLACK TALK CROSSES OVER

> A 16-year-old white Pennsylvanian says his high school is full of "wiggers," whites . . . desperate to adopt black modes of dress and conduct . . . . Call 'em wanna-bes, call 'em rip-offs, call 'em suckers, but they're everywhere—white folks who think they're black. . . . Whites have been riffing off—or ripping off— black cultural forms for more than a century and making a lot more money from them. . . . [Whites] cavalierly adopt . . . the black mantle without having to experience life-long racism, restricted economic opportunity, or any of the thousand insults that characterize black American life. . . . It's a curious spectacle.
>
> —White journalist James Ledbetter
> (staff writer for the *Village Voice*), in
> "Imitation of Life," Fall 1992, *Vibe*
> Magazine

In the nineties U.S.A., the "curious spectacle" is everywhere. White males HOOP on courts in Great Falls, Montana, Oak Park, Illinois, Orange County, California, and Brownsville, Tennessee, HIGH-FIVin it and TALKIN TRASH, often without the slightest inkling that they are doing a BLACK THANG. And they think nothing of donning X caps, wearing them sideways or backwards as is fashionable in the HOOD. White females sport TUDES of twenty-first century assertive womanhood as they RAP "Fly Girl" from Queen Latifah's 1991 album *Nature of [A] Sista*:

> I always hear "Yo, Baby." . . .
> No, my name ain't "Yo,"
> And I ain't got yo "baby."

Coming into their own, white girls issue ultimatums to their WIGGAS, DROPping SCIENCE from Mary J. Blige's 1991 title cut, "What's the 411?":

> The same ol shit you pulled last week on Kim,
> I'm not havin that. . . .
> So come correct with some respect.

A 1993 article by a European American used the title "A New Way to TALK THAT TALK" (small capitals added) to describe a new talk show. *The American Heritage Dictionary,* Third Edition, lists BUG and GRAPEVINE as just plain old words, with no label indicating "slang" or "Black." Merriam-Webster's latest (tenth) edition of its Collegiate Dictionary lists BOOM BOX the same way. A lengthy 1993 article in the *New York Times Magazine,* entitled "Talking Trash," discussed this ancient Black verbal tradition as the "art of conversation in the N.B.A." And in his first year in office, the nation's new "baby boomer" President was taken to task for "terminal HIPness."

The absorption of African American English into Eurocentric

culture masks its true origin and reason for being. It is a language born from a culture of struggle, a way of talking that has taken surviving African language elements as the base for self-expression in an alien tongue. Through various processes such as "Semantic Inversion" (taking words and turning them into their opposites), African Americans stake our claim to the English language, and at the same time, reflect distinct Black values that are often at odds with Eurocentric standards. "Fat," spelled *phat* in Hip Hop, refers to a person or thing that is excellent and desirable, reflecting the traditional African value that human body weight is a good thing, and implicitly rejecting the Euro-American mainstream, where skinny, not fat, is valued and everybody is on a diet. Senior Blacks convey the same value with the expression, "Don't nobody want no BONE." By the process of giving negative words positive meanings, BAD means "good," STUPID means "excellent," and even the word DOPE becomes positive in Hip Hop, meaning "very good" or "superb."

The blunt, coded language of enslavement SIGged ON Christian slaveholders with the expression, "Everybody talkin bout Heaven ain goin there." Hip Hop language, too, is bold and confrontational. It uses obscenities, graphic depictions of the sex act, oral and otherwise, and it adheres to the pronunciation and grammar of African American English (which the uninformed deem "poor English"). Thus B-BOYS and B-girls snub their noses at the European American world and the EUROPEAN NEGRO world as well. About the former, European American journalist Upski, writing from the "front lines of the White Struggle" (in *The Source*, May 1993), says:

> Even lifetime rap fans . . . usually discount a crucial reason rap was invented: white America's economic and psychological terrorism against Black people—reduced in the white mind to "prejudice" and "stereotypes," concepts more within its cultural experience.

About the latter, Armond White, reviewing the 1993 film *CB4* (in *Emerge,* May 1993), writes:

> *CB4* offers an unenlightened view of rap. . . . It panders to . . . the black bourgeois fear that only "proper" language and "civilized" attitudes are acceptable means of addressing politics or articulating personal feelings.

But back to the lecture at hand, as Dr. Dre would say—the crossover of African American Language and Culture. Bemoaned by Black writer Langston Hughes ("they done taken my blues and gone"), reflecting on the out-migration of Black Culture during the Harlem Renaissance era of the 1920s when the "Negro was in vogue" . . . analyzed by white writer Norman Mailer in 1957 in his discussion of the "language of Hip" and "white Negroes" . . . resented, even as I write, by BOO-COOS African Americans, like twenty-two-year-old Jamal, in my survey of Black opinion on the WIGGA phenomenon:

> White folk kill me tryin to talk and be like us; they just want the good part. But it don't go like that; you got to take the bitter with the sweet.

Actually, as I said to the BROTHA, there's plenty of bitter to go around. Contrary to popular Black stereotypes, white folks' life is not all sweetness and light. Despite European Americans' higher material circumstances, it really is true that neither man nor woman can live by bread alone. European Americans live "lives of quiet desperation" too; it's just a different kind of desperation. Which is exactly why Black Talk continues to cross over, doing so today on an unprecedented scale because of the power of post-modern technology.

The dynamism and creativity in African American Language revitalizes and re-energizes bland Euro-talk. There's electricity and excitement in PLAYERS and FLY girls who wear GEAR. The metaphors, images, and poetry in Black Talk make the ordinary ALL THAT, AND THEN SOME. African American English is a

dramatic, potent counterforce to verbal deadness and empti-
ness. One is not simply accepted by a group, one is IN LIKE
FLIN. Fraternities and sororities don't merely march; they perform a STEP SHOW. And when folk get AMP, they don't fight
the feeling, they TESTIFY. For whites, there is a certain magne-
tism in the African American use of English because it seems to
make the impossible possible. I bet you a FAT MAN AGAINST
THE HOLE IN A DOUGHNUT . . . .

For *wiggas* and other white folk latching onto Black Talk,
that's the good news. The bad news is that there's a reality check
in African American English. Its terms and expressions keep you
grounded, catch you just as you are taking flight and bring you
right back down to the NITTY GRITTY of African American
Life. There are rare flights of fancy in this poetry, no chance of
getting so carried away that you don't know yo ASS FROM A
HOLE IN THE GROUND. Unh-unh. Words like NIGGA reinforce
Blackness since, whether used positively, generically, or negatively, the term can refer only to people of African descent.
DEVIL, a negative reference to the white man, reminds Blacks
to be on the lookout for HYPE. RUN AND TELL THAT, historically referring to Blacks who snitched to white folks, is a cul-
tural caution to those planning Black affairs to be wary of the
Judases among them. Such words in the Black Lexicon are con-
stant reminders of race and the Black Struggle. And when you
TALK THAT TALK, you must be loyal to Blackness, or as Ice
Cube would say, be true to the GAME.

There are words and expressions in Black Talk like TWO-
MINUTE BROTHA, describing a man who completes the sex act
in a few seconds, and it's all over for the woman. Both in RAP
and in everyday talk, the words B (bitch) and HO (whore) are
generic references to Black women. GOT HIS/HER NOSE
OPEN describes a male or female so deeply in love that he or she
is ripe for exploitation. Terms like these in Black Language are

continuing reminders that, despite all the talk about Black passion and SOUL, despite all the sixty-minute-man myths, despite all the WOOFin and TALKin SHIT, at bottom, the man-woman Thang among African Americans is just as problematic as it is among other groups.

Some African Americans see crossover as positive because of its possibilities for reducing racial tension. Fashion journalist Robin D. Givhan, writing in the *Detroit Free Press* (June 21, 1993), asserts that she is "optimistic about wiggers":

> Appreciating someone else's culture is good. An increased level of interest among whites in what makes some African Americans groove can only be helpful to improved race relations.

Yet the reality of race, racism, and personal conflicts, which are often intensified by racism, does make crossover problematic. Whites pay no dues, but reap the psychological, social, and economic benefits of a language and culture born out of struggle and hard times. In his "We Use Words Like 'Mackadocious,'" Upski characterizes the "white rap audience" thus: "When they say they like rap, they usually have in mind a *certain* kind of rap, one that spits back what they already believe or lends an escape from their limited lives." And Ledbetter's "Imitation of Life" yields this conclusion: "By listening to rap and tapping into its extramusical expressions, then, whites are attempting to bear witness to—even correct—their own often sterile, oppressive culture." Yet it is also the case that not only Rap, but other forms of Black Language and Culture, are attractive because of the dynamism, creativity, and excitement in these forms. However one accounts for the crossover phenomenon, one thing is certain: today we are witnessing a multi-billion-dollar industry based on this Language-Culture while there is continued underdevelopment and deterioration in the HOOD that produces it. In Ralph Wiley's collection of essays *Why Black People Tend to*

Shout, which contains his *signifyin* piece, "Why Black People Have No Culture," he states: "Black people have no culture because most of it is out on loan to white people. With no interest."

FROM HOME TO HOMEY

You're the kind of girl I wanna get closer to
Become the most to you
Like lovers suppose to do
Cause I fell straight into your trap
And since they say love is blind
I'm the Ray Charles of rap
And I'm waitin for you to put me in ya mix
Because you got my nose open like a jar of Vicks.

—Rapper Big Daddy Kane, "Very Special," from his
1993 album *Looks Like A Job For. . .*

Ray Charles, singer, musician, founder of a seven-piece Rhythm and Blues band . . . born in 1932 . . . blind since age six . . . released his first LP in 1957 . . . soulful style blends Gospel, jazz, blues, and funk . . . height of popularity, the 1960s. Thus Big Daddy Kane and other HIP HOP artists pay tribute to their musical elders and seek to root themselves in The Tradition.

The Mary J. Blige TIP is a soulful blend of Rhythm and Blues, Hip Hop, and 1960s MOTOWN era sounds. This twenty-one-year-old DIVA says that her work "brings people back to those good Old School music days . . . Otis Redding, Gladys Knight, Al Green, Donny Hathaway, the Staple Singers." Guru (gifted/unlimited/rhymes/universal), of the RAP group Gang Starr, had long wanted to JAM with the "old cats." His 1993 album *Jazzmatazz,* which he calls "an experimental fusion of Hip Hop and live jazz," featured Donald Byrd, Roy Ayers, Branford Marsalis, and other jazz greats. Guru KICKS THE BALLISTICS in "Cool Like Us" (*Details,* July 1993):

This is fusion we're doing here. But it's also some gangsta shit. These old cats, they all made records reflecting street life. That's why rappers sample their shit.

Ice Cube's popular JAM "It Was A Good Day" (on his 1992 album *The Predator*) contains samples from the Isley Brothers' "Footsteps in the Dark," on their 1977 album, *Go For Your Guns*. Divas En Vogue went gold with their single "Something He Can Feel," a Curtis Mayfield JAM recorded by Aretha Franklin in the 1970s. Rapper Ice-T paid homage to history when he sold "dope beats and lyrics, no beepers needed" in his "I'm Your Pusher" duet with Mayfield based on Mayfield's 1972 *Superfly* movie soundtrack. Public Enemy (P.E.), always political, protested Arizona's refusal to honor Dr. Martin Luther King, Jr.'s birthday in "By The Time I Get To Arizona" (on their 1991 album *Apocalypse 91: The Enemy Strikes Black*), a Rap that recalls Isaac Hayes's talk-singing jam, "By the Time I Get to Phoenix," on his 1969 *Hot Buttered Soul* album.

SIGNIFYIN, LYIN, TALKIN TRASH, PLAYin THE DOZ-ENS, and other old forms of Black Talk are all over the place today, from GANGSTA Rapper Schooly D's early jam, "Signifyin Rapper," to the recently released HYPE rhymes of Mary J. Blige's "4 1 1" duet with Rapper Grand Puba. Reaching back to Blackness untainted by WANNABE VIBES and the crossover explosion that the 1960s Black Movement set in motion . . . coming correct, with all due respect . . . engaged in a conscious return to The Source . . . making their way toward an African identity for the twenty-first century . . . these HOMEYS are in search of HOME.

Nor is today's generation the first to look for home. Forcibly removed from their native land, homeless Africans in America have been on a continual quest for home since 1619. After Emancipation, they thought they could make home the rich, fertile land of the South. But Reconstruction ended, and the Federal Government abandoned them, forcing them to survive amidst lynch mobs and the Ku Klux Klan and leaving them to fend for themselves as sharecroppers trapped in a new form of enslavement. African Americans began to leave their Southern home in droves, migrating to urban metropolises during and after World Wars I and II. Senior BLOODS and their children of the 1950s and 1960s searched for home in the PROMISED LANDS of the North. But what they found was urban blight, poor housing, inadequate schools, police brutality, and other social problems of the "inner city."

The "deferred dreams" of previous generations exploded in the REBELLIONS of the 1960s. The source of much of Hip Hop's language and many of its cultural forms is the generation that produced these rebellions during the Black Freedom Struggle of the 1960s and 1970s. TLC, the name of a popular female Rap group, is the abbreviation for "tender, loving care"; both the phrase and the abbreviation date back at least to the 1960s and can still be heard in the conversations of those who came of age during that time. Phrases from the 1960s and 1970s, such as BAD *self* and GIT IT ON, are frequently heard when Rappers like P.E. are IN THE HOUSE. Words like JAM and FUNKY are as common in Hip Hop as they were during the 1950s. And when B-BALL star "Sir Charles" Barkley and filmmaker Spike Lee are proudly characterized as "nineties NIGGAZ" (a phrase Barkley himself coined), we are reaching way back to enslavement, when the BAD NIGGA was born. Bad niggaz dared to buck Ole Massa, they didn't TAKE NO SHIT from Blacks or whites, and some of them even lived to tell about it.

Bridging generations, a good deal of Hip Hop lingo recycles either the same word or a variation of an older term. Words like PAD, IG, FRY, and SALTY appeared in Cab Calloway's 1938 *Hepster's Dictionary* and are still current today. Would you prefer to BIG-TIME IT (1960s/1970s) or to LIVE LARGE (1990s)? Answer: either, since both refer to SERIOUS material possessions and living the Good Life. But neither the sixties nor the nineties generation has anything on seniors who convey the same meaning with their colorful expression LIVIN HIGH OFF THE HOG, that is, living as though you're eating the upper parts of the hog, such as ribs or pork chops, rather than the lower parts, such as pig feet or CHITLINS. The PIMP WALK of the 1960s/1970s, the male strutting style of walking with a slight dip in the stride, is essentially the same as the GANGSTA LIMP of the 1990s; both expressions can be heard today. And though neither is identical to the CAT WALK of earlier years, what is important in all of this is the VIBE, the concept of a style of walking that projects a self-assured, TOGETHA, confident, even cocky man-image. Like walking with ATTITUDE . . . like by your walk conveying the message that you GOT IT GOIN ON.

Basic in Black Talk, then, is the commonality that takes us across boundaries. Regardless of job or social position, most African Americans experience some degree of participation in the life of the COMMUNITY — they get their hair done in African American BEAUTY SHOPS, they worship in Black churches, they attend African American social events, and they generally PAR-TAY with Blacks. This creates in-group crossover lingo that is understood and shared by various social groups within the race—words like KINKY and NAPPY to describe the texture of African American hair; HIGH YELLUH to refer to light-complexioned Blacks; CHITLINS to refer to hog intestines, a popular SOUL food; and a ready understanding of the different meanings of the N-WORD.

As stated, the closest connection between generations in Black Talk, as in today's music, is between Hip Hop and the 1960s/1970s. In addition to the terms given above, other examples of parallel expressions include COOL OUT (1960s/1970s) and CHILL (1990s), meaning, to relax, take it calm and easy; DOin IT TO DEF (1960s/1970s) and DEF (1990s), to describe something that is superb or excellent; RUN IT DOWN (1960s/ 1970s) and BREAK IT DOWN (1990s), meaning, to explain and simplify something, make it plain; BLOCK BOY (1960s/1970s) and BANJY BOY (1990s), referring to a gay male in FLY culture who dresses like straight males; ALL THE WAY LIVE (1960s/ 1970s) and LIVE (1990s), to describe an exciting, desirable event, person, place, or experience; and ACE BOON COON (1960s/1970s) and ACE KOOL (1990s), to refer to your best friend.

Another feature of Black Talk is the coining of words that capture unique characteristics of individuals. The older term BOGARD (to aggressively take over something) was based on the style of film star Humphrey Bogart, who typically played strong-arm, tough guy roles. Today's generation has contributed OPRAH to the Lexicon, after talk show personality Oprah Winfrey, to refer to the art of getting people to reveal intimate facts about themselves, as Oprah skillfully manages to do on national television.

African American English had its genesis in enslavement, where it was necessary to have a language that would mean one thing to Africans but another to Europeans. Forced to use the English of Ole Massa, Africans in enslavement had to devise a system of talking to each other about Black affairs and about The MAN right in front of his face. Because of continued segregation and racism, this necessity for a coded form of English persisted even after Emancipation, and it underlies the evolution of Black Language. Black Talk's origin in enslavement and the still-unresolved status of Africans in America account for the constant changes in the Lexicon. If and when a term crosses over into the white world, it becomes suspect and is no longer considered DOPE in the Black world. A new term must be generated to take its place. There is a certain irony here because in this cultural circumstance, imitation is not considered flattery. The same lingo generated by the creative juices of the community and considered DEF today can tomorrow become WACK and suitable only for LAMES if it gets picked up by whites. Of course a lot of African American Talk does get picked up by European Americans, especially in this post-modern nineties era, with MTV, BET, "Def Comedy Jam," and the power of the media to spread culture and language rapidly throughout the nation. Nonetheless, the pattern persists: once phrases and terms are adopted by whites, Blacks scramble to come up with something new.

On the other hand, language that does not cross over, regardless of how old it is, continues to be used in the community and to remain HYPE. Examples include most of the vocabulary of the Traditional Black Church and many of the terms referring to male-female relations. For example, "You GOT my NOSE OPEN" is at least half a century old and was used in Big Daddy Kane's 1993 "Very Special" jam. Another example is WHAM BAM, THANK YOU, MAM! (also BIP BAM, THANK YOU, MAM!), used especially by women to refer to a man who completes the sex act in a matter of seconds; this signifyin expression is also at least fifty years old and was used by Mary J. Blige in her 1992 "4 1 1" jam. Other terms that don't cross over are words for whites, such as ANN, HONKY, CHARLIE; terms referring to Black hair and other physical features, such as ASHY, LIGHT-SKIN, DARK-SKIN, KITCHEN; and other words that describe Blacks only, such as OREO, COLOR STRUCK, TOM.

Though often misunderstood (and even damned) for their NITTY GRITTY language, especially the MUTHAFUCKAS, HO's, and NIGGAZ, the Hip Hop generation is coming straight outa the Oral Tradition. In that Tradition, language is double-voiced, common English words are given unique Black meanings, and a muthafucka is never a person with an Oedipus complex.[8] Rather than breaking with the Black past, as some members of the previous generation have tried to do, Hip Hoppers seek to connect with past verbal traditions and to extend the semantic space of Black lingo by adding a 1990s flavor. They are not merely imitating and reproducing the past, but grounding themselves in it as they seek to stamp their imprint upon the GAME. Any time you venture beyond the tried and true, errors BIG-TIME, painful distortions, and horrific extremes are likely to result. Experimentation breeds failures as well as successes. The violent antagonism toward and brutalization of women by male Rap groups, such as Los Angeles's NWA (Niggaz With Attitudes), is a case in point. But it was also NWA who early on, in their 1989 jam "Fu[ck] the Police," HIPped us to the brutality of the Los Angeles Police Department, which should have prepared us for the Rodney King tragedy had we listened.

This is a historical moment in which Rap and other forms of Black Talk and Culture are used to sell everything from Coca-Cola and Gatorade to snow blowers and shampoo for white hair. When you factor in profits from music, television programming, sports, clothing, and advertising, it is clear that America's corporate economy is capitalizing on Hip Hop, making it a booming billion-dollar industry. However, while Black *Talk* has crossed over, Black *people* have not, as is excruciatingly evident from the staggering unemployment and economic deterioration of the HOOD, reemerging racism (even on college campuses), and open physical attacks on African American males by the police as well as by ordinary white citizens. Recognizing WHAT TIME IT IS, homeys are in search of authentic Black Language and Culture, an unapologetic African American Self, and a way to resolve the unfinished business of being African in America. Their quest has led them to the ruins of the 1960s. There HOMEBOYS and HOMEGIRLS found folk like Rudy Ray Moore's "Dolemite," with his hilarious, pornographic talk and, yes, his put-downs of women. But there they also found the "do-rag lover and revolutionary pimp"[9] Malcolm X.

NOTES

1. The term "Black Freedom Struggle" characterizes the organized mass movement for Black empowerment that began with Mrs. Rosa Parks's now famous refusal to surrender her bus seat to a white man in Montgomery, Alabama, on December 1, 1955. Southern custom required that Blacks sitting in the "Colored" section of a bus give up their seats if the white section was filled. Her unwillingness to do this led to Mrs. Parks's arrest and set in motion the movement that would lead to the eradication of laws supporting racial segregation. The Black Freedom Struggle includes the Civil Rights Movement, led by Dr. Martin Luther King, Jr., and the Black Power Movement, spearheaded by Malcolm X. The terms "Black Liberation Movement" and "Black Movement" are also used to describe this era in the African American Experience. The decline of the Black Freedom Struggle by 1980 is generally attributed to attacks against Black leaders and activists in the form of assassinations (King, Malcolm, Medgar Evers, Fred Hampton, Mark Clark, and others), imprisonment (Angela Davis, Ron Karenga, Reverend Benjamin Chavis, and others), and forced exile (Assata Shakur, Eldridge Cleaver, and others).

2. The "Oral Tradition" refers to stories, old sayings, songs, jokes, proverbs, and other cultural products that have not been written down or recorded. The forms of Oral Tradition cultures are kept alive by being passed on by word of mouth from one generation to the next. The forms reveal the values

and beliefs of the people, the things they hold to be true, and lessons about life and how to live it. Some of the verbal rituals in the African American Oral Tradition involve lengthy narratives about Black superheroes and legendary underdogs that are told in rhyme and go on for literally hours, such as the Toasts "The Signifying Monkey," "Stagolee," and "Shine and the Sinking of the Titanic." Toast-tellers, like other Rappers, must have excellent memories and a way with words.

3. The Republic of New Africa (RNA), an organization founded during the early years of the Black Freedom Struggle, developed the concept of "five states" to be given as reparations to Africans in America for over two centuries of free labor under enslavement. The five states were Alabama, Georgia, Louisiana, Mississippi, and South Carolina. The concept was derived from that of the "Black Belt,"a term referring to the areas of the South where there had historically been the greatest concentration of Blacks (counties with a population 40% or more Black). In the "Black Belt" South, Blacks had lived and worked the land continuously since enslavement. Although the idea was attacked and labeled as "absurd" by the mainstream, it was merely an updating of the "forty acres" provision that the U.S. Congress itself had attempted to make the law of the land in 1866. The RNA vision was that the five states would constitute a sovereign nation that African Americans could call their own, in much the same way that the nation of Israel was created as a form of reparation for Jewish people.

4. The Harlem Renaissance is considered to be an era of great flowering of Black talent in literature, music, and the arts. Also known as the "Negro Renaissance" and the era of "The New Negro," the Harlem Renaissance years were the 1920s. Whites flocked to uptown New York clubs and cabarets to soak up Black Culture, and Harlem was viewed as a cultural mecca. One white writer even celebrated this uptown "para-

dise" with a book entitled *Nigger Heaven*. Many whites also
financially supported struggling Black artists. However, the
impact of this era on the masses of African Americans was
summed up by writer Langston Hughes, himself a member of
the Renaissance literati, who indicated that ordinary Har-
lemites hadn't even heard of the Renaissance, and if they had,
it hadn't "raised their wages any."

5. The Traditional Black Church (TBC) refers to the Protestant
denominational sects, dating back to enslavement, that fused
African styles of worship and beliefs with European American tenets of Christianity. The denominations are the African
Methodist Episcopal Church (A.M.E.), the African Methodist Episcopal Zion Church (A.M.E.Z.), the Christian Methodist Episcopal Church (C.M.E.), the Baptists (the three
groups being the National Baptist Convention, U.S.A., Incor-
porated [NBC], the National Baptist Convention of America,
Unincorporated [NBCA], and the Progressive National Baptist Convention [PNBC]), the Church of God in Christ
(COGIC), the Pentecostal Church, the Holiness Church, and
the Sanctified Church. The worship forms of the TBC include
a belief in spirit-possession, that is, that a person's body can
be taken over by a divine force (the Holy Spirit), expressed by
TALKIN IN TONGUE, holy dancing, shouting, moaning; the
use of up-tempo, passionate music, songs, and musical in-
struments (such as the drum, organ, and guitar); and call-response interaction between preacher and congregation, as
well as between members of the congregation during the service. Historically and down to the present day, the Church
has been a critical institutional force in the liberation, survival, and day-to-day life of Black people. Many slave rebellions were planned in the Church, and there is a history of activist leadership among preachers dating from preacher Nat
Turner, who, in 1831, led what has been deemed the greatest
slave rebellion, to the Reverend Dr. Martin Luther King, Jr.,

leader in the Black Freedom Struggle of the 1960s. Further, the Church has served as an important social unit where there is some kind of activity almost every day of the week and where everyday Black people have opportunities to develop and exercise their abilities in speaking, teaching, singing, organizing, planning, etc. In *The Black Church in the African American Experience,* C. Eric Lincoln and Lawrence H. Mamiya sum it up this way:

> The Black Church has no challenger as the cultural womb of the black community. Not only did it give birth to new institutions such as schools, banks, insurance companies, and low income housing, it also provided an academy and an arena for political activities, and it nurtured young talent for musical, dramatic, and artistic development . . . . Multifarious levels of community involvement [are] found in the Black Church, in addition to the traditional concerns of worship, moral nurture, education, and social control. Much of black culture is heavily indebted to the black religious tradition, including most forms of black music, drama, literature, storytelling, and even humor.

6. Throughout this Introduction and in the dictionary that follows, I use both the labels "European American" and "white" to refer to Americans of European descent in the United States, just as I use the labels "African American" and "Black" to refer to Americans of African descent in the U. S. Readers will note that "Black" is capitalized whereas "white" is not. First, *Black* as a racial designation replaced *Negro,* and *Negro* was capitalized (at least since 1930), whereas *white* was not. Second, for people of African descent in America, *Black* functions to designate race *and* ethnicity because the slave trade and U. S. enslavement practices made it impossible for "Blacks" to trace their ethnic origins in Africa. This has not been the case for Europeans in the U.S.,

who typically have labelled themselves German, Italian, English, Irish, Polish, etc., according to their European ethnicity. In fact, it was not until the rise of *Black* that European Americans raised questions about the lower-casing of *white*.

7. Although Republican Rutherford B. Hayes had not won the popular vote in the Presidential race of 1876, nonetheless he became President over his Democratic opponent, Samuel J. Tilden. At this time during Reconstruction, the nation was in economic and social turmoil, and the former enslaved African population was at the center of the bitter political conflict between the country's white Democrats and Republicans. The Republican Party at that time was the political party of choice for the "freedmen," who had placed their hopes for equity and parity in the party that maintained Federal troops to protect Black voting rights and stem white violence against Blacks. However, as historian John Hope Franklin put it in his *From Slavery to Freedom:* "The Democrats were committed to a program to end Reconstruction in the South; the Republicans had not openly promised to do so, but there was at least one wing of the party that was willing to withdraw troops and leave the South to its own devices." The Presidential vote was disputed in South Carolina, Louisiana, and Florida, in what Franklin calls "the three states that had not been 'redeemed,'" and in the case of South Carolina and Louisiana, where dual governments had been set up. Thus, the race between Tilden and Hayes had to be decided by a count of the electoral votes and the results certified by both Houses of Congress. Although the Election Commission sustained Hayes's claim to the Presidency, Democrats, who were in the majority in the House of Representatives, instituted a filibuster to prevent the certification of the Election Commission's results. Their objective was to create chaos by filibustering until Inauguration Day, in which case, as historian Lerone Bennett, Jr., put it in his *Before the Mayflower,* ". . . America

would not have a President. And disorder, perhaps war, would be inevitable." Hayes and his boys, however, wanted the Presidency badly, and so in back rooms of the nation's capital, a deal was cut. Bennett writes:

> Representatives of Hayes and representatives of the South huddled together in smoky rooms. The price—that was the question. How much? The South wanted certain economic concessions, but most of all it wanted "home rule": the right to deal with the Negro in its own way, a suspension, in fact, of constitutional safeguards which protected the Negro. *Quid pro quo*—something for something. "Home Rule" for the South, withdrawal of troops, an end to agitation of the Negro question, a tacit agreement that the South would be allowed to deal with the Negro in its own way. And for Hayes? The Presidency.

8. The Oedipus complex derives from the work of Sigmund Freud (1856–1939), the Austrian physician who founded psychoanalysis. This theory of human behavior argues that psychological problems are traceable to infancy and childhood and the individual's failure to resolve childhood sexual conflicts and fantasies, which should come about naturally with maturity. One such conflict is the sexual desire of a male child for his mother and subsequent hostility toward his father, who is enjoying the sexual pleasures denied the child. This problem was named the "Oedipus complex" after the character Oedipus in Greek mythology. He was abandoned at birth and wandered to and fro until adulthood, when fate led him to Thebes, where he killed the king and married the queen, who, unbeknownst to Oedipus (or them), were his parents.

9. From the poem "Malcolm Spoke/who listened? (this poem is for my consciousness too)," by Haki Madhubuti, from his collection *Don't Cry, Scream,* published in 1969, when he was Don L. Lee.

SELECTED
REFERENCES

Alleyne, Mervyn. *Comparative Afro-American.* Ann Arbor, Mich.: Karoma Publishers, 1980.

Asante, Molefi Kete. "African Elements in African American English." In *Africanisms in American Culture,* edited by Joseph Holloway. Bloomington: Indiana University Press, 1990.

Baugh, John. *Black Street Speech: Its History, Structure, and Survival.* Austin: University of Texas Press, 1983.

Bennett, Lerone, Jr. *Before the Mayflower: A History of Black America.* Chicago: Johnson Publishing Company, 1969.

Blassingame, John. *The Slave Community: Plantation Life in the Antebellum South.* New York: Oxford University Press, 1979.

Botkin, B. A., ed. *Lay My Burden Down: A Folk History of Slavery.* Chicago: University of Chicago Press, 1945.

Dalby, David. *Black Through White: Patterns of Communication in Africa and the New World.* Bloomington: Indiana University Press, 1969.

Dawsey, Darrell. "Debating the N-Word." *Emerge,* June 1993, 35–36.

Dillard, J. L. *Black English.* New York: Random House, 1972.

DuBois, W. E. B. *Souls of Black Folk.* 2nd ed. New York: Vintage Books/Library of America, 1990. First published in 1903.

Franklin, John Hope. *Reconstruction: After the Civil War.* Chicago: University of Chicago Press, 1961.

Gilyard, Keith. *Voices of the Self.* Detroit: Wayne State University Press, 1991.

Herskovits, Melville. *The Myth of the Negro Past.* Boston: Beacon Press, 1941.

Kochman, Thomas. *Black and White Styles in Conflict.* Chicago: University of Chicago Press, 1981.

Krapp, George Philip. *The English Language in America.* New York: Modern Language Association, 1925.

Labov, William. *Language in the Inner City: Studies in the Black English Vernacular.* Philadelphia: University of Pennsylvania Press, 1972.

Lincoln, C. Eric, and Lawrence H. Mamiya. *The Black Church in the African American Experience.* Durham: Duke University Press, 1990.

McDavid, R. I., and V. G. McDavid. "The Relationship of the Speech of American Negroes to the Speech of Whites." *American Speech* 26 (February 1951): 3–17.

Smitherman, Geneva. *Talkin and Testifyin: The Language of Black America.* Detroit: Wayne State University Press, 1986.

———. " 'What is Africa to Me?': Language Ideology and African American." *American Speech* 66 (Summer 1991): 115–132. Reprinted in *Word: A Black Culture Journal,* Winter 1993, and in *African American Communications: A Reader in Traditional and Contemporary Studies,* edited by James W. Ward, Kendall Hunt, Dubuque, Iowa, 1992. [A survey of Blacks in five cities on the name change from "Black" to "African American." The cities were Atlanta, Chicago, Cincinnati, Philadelphia, and Detroit.]

———. "Survey of African American Opinion on the Use of Nigga and Wigga." In progress; forthcoming, 1994.

Stuckey, Sterling. "Identity and Ideology: The Names Controversy." In *Slave Culture: Nationalist Theory and the Foundations of Slavery.* New York: Oxford University Press, 1987.

Taylor, Hanni U. *Standard English, Black English, and Bidialectalism: A Controversy.* New York: P. Lang, 1989.

Turner, Lorenzo. *Africanisms in the Gullah Dialect.* Chicago: University of Chicago Press, 1949.

Wiley, Ralph. *Why Black People Tend to Shout.* New York: Penguin Books, 1992.

Wolfram, Walter, and Nona H. Clarke, eds. *Black-White Speech Relationships.* Washington: Center for Applied Linguistics, 1971.

Woodson, Carter G. *The Miseducation of the Negro.* Washington: Associated Publishers, 1933.

EXPLANATORY
NOTES

❖ ❖ ❖ ❖ ❖

The language of African Americans has been given a variety of names: Black English, Ebonics, Black Talk, African American Vernacular English, Black Dialect, Ghetto Speech, Street Talk, and others. This dictionary uses the terms "African American English" and "Black Talk." Often, when people refer to the words and phrases in African American English, they use the term "slang." Although Black Talk includes slang, it is much more inclusive and expansive than that label suggests. For one thing, slang refers to language that is transitory and that is generally used by only one group, such as teenagers' slang or musicians' slang. African American English, however, has a lexical core of words and phrases that are fairly stable over time and are familiar to and/or used by all groups in the Black community. This dictionary attempts to capture the essence of this lexical core. (See Introduction for a fuller discussion of this commonality in Black Talk.)

All of the words/phrases in this dictionary are in current use by Blacks from all walks of life: blue- and white-collar workers, professionals and businessmen/women, preachers and other church folk, Hip Hoppers, political activists, musicians, hustlers and gangstas, senior citizens. Some words/phrases are more common in one context than another—that is, in the Traditional Black Church, or in Hip Hop Culture, or among Black women. The particular context is indicated in the definitions and examples that accompany such words/phrases.

Several methods were used in compiling this dictionary. Some words/phrases are from written language surveys and word lists completed by Black people from various age and social groups around the country. Other words/phrases were gathered from songs, hit recordings, and films. Still others were gathered using ethnographic methods: participating in and observing conversations and speakers; conducting informal face-to-face interviews; collecting words/phrases from community bulletins, leaflets, meetings, announcements, handwritten notes and letters, call-ins to radio programs; and occasionally even eavesdropping. In general, formal written or published sources were not consulted, and no words/phrases are included that have appeared only in formal writing. The various illustrative sentences accompanying the definitions are the actual spoken words of Africans in America.

Of course, what we linguists call my "native speaker competence," as a daughter of the hood who continues to live and socialize there, was very useful in pulling together this dictionary. However, no word/phrase is included whose use could not be verified by several Black speakers.

Unlike standard dictionaries, the definitions here do not usually include the origin, or etymological history, of a word/phrase, nor is there any attempt to identify who first used a word/phrase—these are risky propositions at best when dealing with an oral language such as African American English. Instead, since Black Talk can be fully understood only within the Black context, this dictionary concentrates on the historical and contemporary significance of words/phrases in the context of African American Culture and the Black Experience. Such explanatory details accompany many of the definitions.

In many words/phrases in Black Talk, the authentic Black sound depends on use of the African American English system of grammar and pronunciation. (Some of the rules governing this system are explained in the Introduction.) Where the authentic Black sound is important, a word/phrase is listed with the spelling that most closely approximates that sound. In some instances, the African American English spelling produces a word that appears to be the same as an altogether different word in formal written English. Such words/phrases are listed with both the formal written spelling and the spelling that conveys Black Talk, but the definition is given only at the entry under the Black pronunciation.

If a word/phrase used in a definition appears in small capitals, it is listed elsewhere in the dictionary.

"Also" is used to indicate a word/phrase that is a synonym or near equivalent. "See also" is used to refer to words/phrases that will provide further information. Words and phrases following "Also" and "See also" appear in italics.

"Crossover" refers to a word/phrase in Black Talk that has moved beyond the African American context and is now in general use by European Americans. Some crossover words/phrases are linked to African languages and have become so common in American speech that most people are unaware of their origin. (The African background of African American English is discussed in the Introduction. Interested readers should also consult the references given there for more information on this aspect of Black Talk.) In many cases, however, the linguistic origin of crossover words/phrases is unknown. Such words/phrases were (and still are) used widely in the African American community before they entered into more general use among European Americans.

A

A AND B

Two musical selections by a Gospel singer or group during a church service or on a musical program. "The mass choir is being asked to give an A and B on Sunday afternoon's program."

A AND B CONVERSATION

A discussion or conversation between two people. A third party interfering is told, "This is an A and B conversation, and you can C yo way out of it." See also DIPPIN.

ABOUT

See BE BOUT.

ACE BOON COON

Best friend. Also *ace kool* (newer term).

ACE KOOL

See ACE BOON COON (older term).

AFRAAMERICAN

See AFRICAN AMERICAN.

AFRIAMERICAN

See AFRICAN AMERICAN.

AFRICAN

1) In the vocabulary of activist and AFRICAN-CENTERED Blacks, any person of African descent in the DIASPORA — Black American, Jamaican, Haitian, etc.—not limited to Continental Africans; when written, may be spelled *Afrikan*. 2) The name used by enslaved Africans to refer to themselves and their churches and organizations from 1619 until roughly 1800. See Introduction. 3) In the vocabulary of working-class Blacks and the Black so-called "masses," used primarily to refer to Continental Africans.

AFRICAN AMERICAN

A person of African descent, born in and a citizen of the United States, whose U.S. ancestry dates back to the enslavement era—i.e., a Black American, as distinguished from a Jamaican, Haitian, or other Diasporic African. The term has been in widespread usage since about 1988, but was also used, to some extent, during the 1960s (as well as during the nineteenth century). Writing it with a hyphen may trigger resentment among some Blacks since other U.S. ethnic group names are now generally represented without a hyphen, such as Asian American, Hispanic (or Latino/Latina) American, Italian American, etc. Also *AfriAmerican, AfraAmerican*. See Introduction.

AFRICAN-CENTERED

1) Refers to a person, event, or operation that is focused on Africans and African Americans. 2) Refers to a perspective in which Blackness and Africa are the center, focus, or subject, rather than the object.

AFRICAN HOLOCAUST

An emerging term among writers, Rappers, and Black activists to refer to the enslavement of African people in the United States and throughout the DIASPORA. It captures the experience of the wholesale destruction of a group of people and the consequences, yet to be assessed, of the *African holocaust* on present-day Black communities. Estimates of the number of Africans forcibly removed from their native lands during the European slave trade range as high as one hundred million, not all of whom reached the so-called "New World." Millions of Africans perished as a result of torture, disease, and the horrendous Middle Passage across the Atlantic Ocean. Thousands committed suicide.

AFRICAN PEOPLE'S TIME

A reference to the African/African American concept of

time, being in tune with human events, nature, the seasons, and natural rhythms, as opposed to being a slave to the clock, which represents artificial, rather than natural, time. Being "in time," that is, in tune with experience, emotions, feelings, the general flow of things, is more critical than being "on time." Also *CPT, CP Time, Colored People's Time.*

AFRIKAN

See AFRICAN.

AFRO

A hairstyle that is natural, not straightened, trimmed along the hairline, and worn full and thick or thin and cropped close to the head. Highly popular among both females and males during the 1960s and 1970s; not as widespread in the 1990s, but still worn to some extent, especially by females. Also *fro.*

AFROAMERICAN

See AFRICAN AMERICAN. *AfroAmerican* is not as widespread today as *African American*; used during the 1960s and 1970s, as well as during the nineteenth and early twentieth centuries. See Introduction.

AFRO-SAXON

See EUROPEAN NEGRO (newer term). *Afro-Saxon* is believed to have been coined by Continental Africans in the 1970s. However, the term also relates to the title of a 1965 book, *The Black Anglo-Saxons,* a widely discussed critique of the Black American middle and professional classes, by sociologist and clinical psychologist Dr. Nathan Hare, a former Howard University professor and founder of the first African American Studies department (at San Francisco State University in 1968).

AFTER-HOUR JOINT

A place where people party, as well as gamble, drink, or do drugs, after the official closing of bars and clubs. Operated illegally, with prices substantially above those of legitimate entertainment places.

AIRISH

Cool and breezy. "It seems a mite airish out here."

AK

An AK-47 assault rifle. "Today I didn't even have to use my AK./I gotta say it was a good day" (the Rapper Ice Cube, on his 1992 album *The Predator*). The original AK was a Soviet-designed weapon; the Chinese version was exported to the United States. During the Bush administration, its import for civilian use was outlawed, and prices jumped up due to limited availability. However, AKs can still be purchased legally in gun stores for $300–$550 and in the street, in both semi-automatic and automatic conversion forms, at fluctuating prices, anywhere from $100–$1,000.

ALL IS WELL

An expression used to indicate that a person has been in a bad or threatening situation, but that everything is now okay.

ALL THAT

Excellent, fantastic, superb—all that something or someone appears to be. "The Sista is bad; she is definitely all that."

ALL THAT, AND THEN SOME

Even better than ALL THAT.

ALL THE WAY LIVE

Describes an extremely lively, exciting, desirable event, person, place, or experience. "My boy was all the way live at that concert!" Also *live* (newer form).

ALL THE WAY THROUGH

1) Totally exasperated with someone or something. 2) Totally outdone, emotionally exhausted, taken aback by an action or statement. Also *too through*. See also THROUGH.

ALLEY BALL

Basketball played in urban HOODS. Derived from the older practice of HOOPing in urban areas by attaching the net to the back of a building or a garage (located in the back of the house in many older urban areas). The paved concrete alley becomes the "court." In urban areas, alleys are often used to store garbage and trash for collection by dump trucks.

AMEN CORNER

1) In the Traditional Black Church (TBC), originally the place where the older members sit, especially older women, the Church "mothers," who are perceived as the "watchdogs of Christ" and who often lead the congregation in responsive *Amen*s. 2) Any section of the Church where the congregation uses many verbal responses and *Amen*s. 3) By extension, outside the Church world, a reference to any area where there are expressions of strong support and high feeling for a speaker or performer.

AMP

Stirred up; in a heightened emotional state. From the shortened way of referring to a stereo amplifier, which magnifies, heightens, "stirs up" the sound. From Public Enemy's "Fight the Power," on their 1990 album *Fear of a Black Planet*: "I'm ready and . . . amp,/Most of my heroes don't appear on no stamps." Also *geek, geek up* (older terms).

AND YOU KNOW THAT!

An expression of agreement; a reaffirmation of something that's been said.

ANGEL DUST

Phencyclidine (PCP), an animal tranquilizer, used as an illegal drug that has a hallucinogenic effect. Used as an "upper" in the 1960s and 1970s; perceived by Blacks as a "HONKY Thang," i.e., a drug more commonly used by whites than Blacks. The term, which has now crossed over into general U.S. slang, probably derived from the African American way of describing the effect of the drug: "That shit [*angel dust*] dem honkies be usin put you up there with the angels." Also *PCP*.

ANKH

A T-shaped cross with a loop on top, symbolizing fertility and life; a popular African artifact, worn as jewelry.

ANN

1) Any white woman; used derisively. 2) By extension, used to refer to any uppity-acting Black woman, especially one who "acts white." Also *Miss Ann*.

APPLAUSE

Gonorrhea. Derived from older term "the clap."

THE APPLE

New York City. Also *the Big Apple*. The term originated with early African American jazz musicians; now a cross-over term.

APPLE

A man's hat with an exceptionally wide brim, stylish in the 1960s and 1970s; from the APPLE, by association with the bigness of New York City.

A-RAB

An Arabic person. Pronounced AY-rab. Some Arab Americans mistakenly think that *A-rab* is a different word from "Arab," and that it was coined by Blacks to CALL Arabs OUTA THEY NAME. This has become an especially sensitive point in places where there are large numbers of Arabs, such as Michigan, which has the largest concentration of Arab Americans in the United States. However, *A-rab* is not a unique "Black word," but a Black pronunciation. Nor is it a racial epithet. It merely reflects the way African Americans speak English, in this instance, probably modeled on such African American English pronunciations as HO-tel, MO-tel, PO-lice, E-light, DE-troit. See Introduction.

ARE YOU RIGHT?

1) A Traditional Black Church phrase, raising a question about one's spiritual status, that is, "Are you saved? Are you right with God?" 2) By extension, used outside the Church (as are many TBC terms and expressions) to refer to a person's moral status, that is, "Are you honest and principled? Do you have good intentions?" The Sista said, "I asked the nigga was he right? Cause if he ain't, he better git right befoe he come up in here!"

AROUND THE WAY

1) Describes somebody from the HOOD. "I need an around the way girl." 2) In the near vicinity. "I just saw her around the way."

AS GOD IS MY SECRET JUDGE

An expression commonly used to affirm the truth of or to prove one's assertion. "As God is my secret judge, I didn bus on the Brotha."

ASHY

Describes the whitish or grayish appearance of skin due to exposure to wind and cold; shows up more on African Americans than European Americans due to Black people's darker skin pigmentation.

ASS¹

Added after a word to give the description extra emphasis. "He is a wor-some-ass man, I know that much," meaning, The man is a pest, always bothering people, either to talk or to get special favors from them.

ASS²

Used after YO, my, etc., to refer to punishment or some form of retribution that is likely to result from one's action or inaction. "If you mess up this time, it's yo ass." Cross-over meaning.

ASS FROM A HOLE IN THE GROUND
Refers to a person pretending to have knowledge, especially a "know-it-all" who doesn't have MOTHER WIT and cannot make fine, discriminating judgments. "He up there runnin his mouth and don't know his ass from a hole in the ground." Crossover expression. Also SHIT FROM SHINOLA.

ASS ON ONE'S SHOULDER
Refers to a person acting arrogant, displaying a TUDE. "We was tryin to talk to him, but he had his ass on his shoulder."

ATTITUDE
See TUDE. *Attitude* has crossed over, but *tude* has not.

AUDI 5000
See OUTTIE 5000. Also *outa here* (newer term); *Later* (older term).

AUNT HAGAR'S CHILLUN
Older term for AFRICAN AMERICANS.

AUNT JANE
An African American woman who identifies more with the European American race than her own, does not support Black causes, and may even work against such causes. Also *Aunt Thomasina.*

AUNT THOMASINA
See AUNT JANE.

B

B

1) A form of address for a male or female, though more common for males; probably a shortened form of BLOOD. "Yo B, whassup?" Sometimes the initial of the person's first name is substituted for "B." 2) Euphemism for BITCH.

B-BALL[1]

The game of basketball. Also *hoop.*

B-BALL[2]

To play basketball. Also *hoop, shoot some hoop.*

B-BOY

A male follower of HIP HOP. Originally (in the Bronx and Harlem in the 1970s) *B-boys* referred to BROTHAS who would regularly "break" out into a dance movement in response to the DJ's scratching of a record. The term *B-boy* is believed to have been coined by the entertainer Kool DJ Herc. "Break" dancing, a rhythmic, intense type of dancing, with twirls, turns, and intricate, fancy steps, is rooted in African and Caribbean dance movements.

BABY

A form of address for a male or female. "Hey baby, whassup?" Between males, the term shows solidarity and close

mission of the artist, Craig Rex Perry, and *Young Sisters and Brothers Magazine.*

friendship, as well as security about masculinity. That is, the man who uses it is secure enough about his manhood that he can address another man as *baby* (this male-to-male usage is on the decline).

BABY FACTORY

Used with reference to a woman who has had a lot of children. "What she got over there—a baby factory?"

BABY GIRL

A form of address for a female, usually one younger than the person speaking. Conveys solidarity and closeness. Also *baby sis*.

BABY SIS

See BABY GIRL.

BACK

A woman's buttocks; if round and large in proportion to a woman's body, viewed as sexy. Also *behind, boody* (older terms); *bumper kit* (newer term).

BACKING THE NUMBERS

See NUMBERS.

BAD

1) Good, excellent, great, fine. From the Mandingo language in West Africa, *a ka nyi ko-jugu,* literally, "It is good badly," meaning, "It is very good," that is, so good that it is *bad*. See Introduction. Crossover use. 2) Powerful, tough, aggressive, fearless. This meaning has not crossed over.

BAD HAIR

Hair that is naturally tightly curled (KINKY, NAPPY), not straight. A negative expression; in this instance, *bad* means "not good." AFRICAN-CENTERED people and political activists reject this view. See also GOOD HAIR.

BAD MOUTH

1) To DIS and/or gossip about a person. 2) To talk negatively about a thing. From Mandingo *da jugu,* "slander, abuse," literally, "bad mouth." Crossover expression.

BAD NIGGA

An African American, generally male, who is rebellious, aggressive, and refuses to succumb to the oppression of the dominant Euro-American culture; one who "doan TAKE no SHIT from nobody, Black or white."

BAG

1) A person's activities, area of specialization, or preference. 2) A person involved in the drug trade is said to have the *bag* or to be the *bag* man/woman. 3) A quantity of marijuana or other drug, such as a DIME *bag*, NICKEL *bag*, etc. Crossover meaning.

BAIL

To leave.

BAILIN

Posting bail to get out of jail; implies that it's a regular occurrence for the person.

BALL[1]

The basketball used in B-BALL.

BALL[2]

1) To play basketball. 2) To dance, BALLROOM style.

BALLER

A large-scale, big-time crack dealer. More frequent in Los Angeles gang talk. See also BALLIN.

BALLIN

1) Playing basketball superbly. 2) Accumulating large sums of money by selling crack (and other drugs).

BALLISTICS

Facts, data. "KICK the *ballistics,*" meaning, Inform us, enlighten us, present the factual information.

BALLROOM

An elaborate slow dance in which the couple glides all over the dance floor.

BANGER

A member of a gang. Also *gangbanger.*

BANGIN

   1) Participating in a gang and all its activities. Also *gang-bangin*. 2) Having sex. 3) Fighting.

BANJY BOY

   A gay male in the HIP HOP Culture who dresses like the straight males in Hip Hop. Also *block boy* (older term).

BANK¹

   A large sum of money. Someone who always has money is said to "keep plenty of *bank*."

BANK²

   To make money, in any amount that the person considers to be a lot.

BANKROLL

   A large amount of money, or at least what appears to be a large amount, carried by a person; however, see PHILLY/ PHILADELPHIA BANKROLL.

BAREFOOT AS A RIVER DUCK

   Describes a person walking around without any shoes on.

BARS

   Rims on a car, in flashy colors and designs, as in the popular HAMMER, a car with gold and chrome rims. It costs from five to six thousand dollars for four rims.

BASE

   1) To use cocaine by heating it with other ingredients and smoking it in a large pipe. Also *freebase*. Since the introduction and widespread use of crack, a form of cocaine that is cheaper and already cooked up for the SMOKER, *basin* has declined in popularity. 2) To criticize or talk harshly to someone. "Look, man, you don't have to base like that. I'm just tryin to help you."

BASEHEAD

   A person addicted to FREEBASin cocaine. The term and use are on the decline. Now users of cocaine are SMOKIN it in the derivative form, crack, and are called CRACKHEADS.

BE ABOUT

See BE BOUT.

BE BOUT

To do something or to be involved in doing something, especially something meaningful. "Them Sistas in the hood is bout the people's business."

BE SOMEBODY

To make something productive or positive out of one's life. Probably from the Reverend Jesse Jackson's well-known call to Black audiences, "I am somebody," to which audiences respond by repeating the statement. See Introduction.

BEAM ON

To gaze intently at a person; to stare. "I saw you beamin on my girl, man. I don't play that."

BEAM UP

To get high on drugs. Probably derived from the television program "Star Trek," where Kirk and company are "beamed up" to distant places in the universe.

BEAMER

A BMW automobile. Also *Five Hundred*.

BEAR

An ugly, unattractive person. Also *booguh-bear*.

BEAR WITNESS

To attest to an experience, fact, or event. Often, but not necessarily, used in reference to a religious experience.

BEAST

A derogatory term for a white person, especially a white male.

BEASTLY

Ugly.

BEAT DOWN[1]

A beating. "If she keep gittin up in my face, she gon catch a beat down."

BEAT DOWN[2]

To fight a person; to beat somebody up badly.

BEAUCOUP

See BOO-COOS.

BEAUTICIAN

A term commonly used by senior African American women to refer to their hairdresser.

BEAUTY SHOP

A place where women get their hair done—and often a gathering place where women rap, debate, discuss, network, TALK SHIT, and provide support for each other.

BÉ-BÉ KID (PRONOUNCED BAY-BAY)

An undisciplined, unruly child who "acts out." The concept was created by the late Robin Harris, the popular comic genius, who also starred in the cartoon movie *Bé-Bé's Kids*. The term was originally associated with children of single, low-income African American mothers, who are often perceived as neglecting their kids and leaving them to raise themselves, as Harris portrayed his *Bé-Bé's kids*. However, the term quickly expanded to refer to *any* disruptive child who acts outrageous, is disobedient, and does what he/she wants to do.

BE-BOP

See BOP¹.

BEEF

Penis.

BEES

That's how it is, that's the way it goes, that's life; an existential reference to the human condition. Also *bees dat way*. Also spelled *bes, be's, bee's*.

BEES DAT WAY
  See BEES.

BEHIND
  Used to refer to a woman's buttocks. See BACK.

BENZ
  A Mercedes Benz automobile. Also *Benzo*.

BENZO
  See BENZ.

BET
  An affirmative response, meaning "All right," "Yes,"
  "Okay."

BID
  A popular card game, played by four people coupled off as
  partners. A traditional social event with verbal rituals and
  social conventions; provides an opportunity for competi-
  tors to display skill in SIGNIFYIN, LYIN, and other features
  of the African American Verbal Tradition. Also *Bid Whis*,
  Whis.

BID
  1) To state the number of books over six that one expects to
  win in the game of BID; also, the number stated itself, that
  is, the *bid*. 2) A prison sentence; the amount of time one has
  to do. For example, a "skid *bid*" is a light sentence. See also
  DO A BID.

BID WHIS
  See BID.

BIDDY
  A teenage female. Also *bitty*.

BIDNESS
  Any personal affair, event, experience, or activity one is involved in. "I got some bidness to take care of" might refer
  to anything from paying a utility bill to confronting somebody about a deal that's gone awry. *Bidness* is the AAE pro-

nunciation of "business." See also PUT SOMEBODY'S BIDNESS IN THE STREET, TAKE CARE OF BIDNESS.

BIG
Pregnant.

THE BIG APPLE
See the APPLE.

BIG D
See D.

BIG FOE
Hard-core, tough, usually big, urban police detectives given wide latitude and unchecked discretion to investigate organized crime, such as gambling, prostitution, ROLLIN, NUMBERS, etc. Resented—and feared—throughout the community because of their brutality, their arrogant policing style in the HOOD, and their assumption that all citizens in the hood are criminals. The term is derived from the older practice of assigning four detectives to a car. *Foe* is the AAE pronunciation of "four"; see Introduction.

BIG FOUR
See BIG FOE.

BIG FUN
An exceptionally good time, generally in reference to a party or social event.

BIG LIPS
A derogatory reference to a person's large, full mouth. Also *thick lips*. An older term reflecting rejection of African American physical features, a view out of step with today's fashion and beauty trends. The *big-lipped* look is now sought after, with women whose lips are Euro thin applying heavy lipstick to create the illusion of thick lips.

BIG MOMMA
1) Grandmother. 2) An affectionate form of address for a stout woman.

BIG PAPER
> A lot of money. Also *tall paper.*

BIG-TIME
> Added after a word to indicate "very much, extremely."
> "You busy big-time," that is, You are extremely busy.

BIG-TIMIN IT
> See LIVIN HIGH OFF THE HOG.

BILL
> A hundred dollars, either in several small bills or a single
> hundred-dollar bill. Crossover term.

BIP BAM, THANK YOU, MAM!
> 1) A SIGNIFYIN expression used especially by women to
> refer to a man who completes the sex act in a matter of sec-
> onds, and it's all over for the woman. 2) By extension, any
> quick, premature action or behavior. Older phrase resurfac-
> ing. Also *Wham bam, thank you, Mam!*

BITCH
> 1) A generic term for any female. Though not always used
> with a negative meaning, it is generally considered negative
> when used by males. However, women use the term among
> themselves. This generic use of *bitch* is occurring with in-
> creasing frequency among female RAP groups, such as Le-
> Shaun and Nikki D (described as "some of the best talent in
> today's hardcore hip hop"). LeShaun: "'93 is the year for
> bitches. . . . Look at us, look at the talent around this ta-
> ble . . ." Nikki D: "It ain't like we hate niggas [i.e., Black
> men]. We love 'em . . . but bitches gotta get down with one
> another just like men do. . . . We've got to come together"
> (from *The Source,* June 1993). 2) Used by males or females
> to refer to a weak or subservient male. 3) In basketball or
> other competitive games, players may use the term to unset-
> tle their opponents so they'll lose their COOL —and the
> game. Also *B* (euphemism).

BITE

1) To give exaggerated praise to someone; to ingratiate one-self in order to receive something from someone. The person who does this is said to be *biting*. 2) To copy a style, a look, a behavior. "After seeing Mary J. Blige in concert, they ran out to the mall to bite the look." 3) To vigorously and intensely work vaginal muscles during lovemaking, producing a sensation men describe as *biting*. See also SNAPPER.

BITING

See BITE.

BITTY

See BIDDY.

BK

1) Any Burger King restaurant. "She's a BK Mademoiselle, wrinkly uniform and bottom bell and some jelly stuff on her sleeve" (from the RAP group De La Soul's "Bitties in the BK Lounge," on their 1991 album *De La Soul Is Dead*). 2) Black Killers, a Midwestern gang, no longer in existence.

BLACK

1) Interchangeable with AFRICAN AMERICAN. Still preferred by some Blacks and widely used, but *African American* is becoming the label of choice. Likely to trigger resentment if not capitalized. Before the late 1960s, considered a negative term. See Introduction. 2) A form of address, as in "Yo, Black" or "Whassup, Black?" 3) Refers to any person of African descent anywhere in the world.

BLACK AND TAN

Any bar or place of entertainment catering to African Americans. An older term derived from a reference to dark ("black") and light ("tan") complexions among Blacks.

BLACK BOTTOM

One of the areas in Detroit where large numbers of Blacks,

of all social classes, were concentrated during the 1920s through the end of World War II. In the early years it was a thriving, bustling center of African American businesses, upscale entertainment, and stable schools and neighborhoods. With continued overcrowding, housing segregation, and the eventual flight of middle-class Blacks, *Black Bottom* came to be perceived as a "ghetto slum" by the 1950s. See also BOTTOM.

BLACK THANG
A reference to any cultural or social practice, behavior, or attitude unique to or stemming from the African American Experience.

BLACKER THAN THOU
A SIGNIFYIN expression used to refer to an African American who thinks he/she sets the standard for Blackness and DISSES other African Americans for not acting or thinking "Black enough."

THE BLACKER THE BERRY, THE SWEETER THE JUICE
An age-old proverb, referring to the power and desirability of Black skin color; resurfacing in HIP HOP. A variation is used in a slogan to support historically Black colleges: "The Blacker the college, the sweeter the knowledge."

BLESSED
A Traditional Black Church term referring to a person who has confessed to and been rescued from his/her sins and is now a devout follower of Christ. Pronounced bles-SED. See also SAVED.

BLOB
See SLOB.

BLOCK
To interfere with a man who's HITTIN ON—i.e., trying to establish a relationship with—a woman. Euphemism for

cock block. A man who does this is said to be a *cock blocker.*

BLOCK BOY

See BANJY BOY (newer term).

BLONDIE

A negative term for a white female.

BLOOD

1) A generic term for any person of African descent; a positive term, noting the genetic kinship and shared bloodlines of African people. 2) A member of the Los Angeles gang the BLOODS.

BLOODS

The name of a gang in Los Angeles. By the end of the 1980s, the *Bloods* and the CRIPS, a rival L.A. gang, had spread and set up outposts in other cities, and thus received some media attention during 1990. The role of the gangs in the 1992 Los Angeles REBELLION (triggered by the "not guilty" verdict for the police officers in the Rodney King beating) and their truce and participation in efforts to heal and rebuild Los Angeles have made the *Crips* and *Bloods* almost household words in the COMMUNITY.

BLOW[1]

1) To sing, play an instrument, or RAP exceptionally well; to achieve excellence in one's work. "Aretha, Quincy, P.E.—now them Bloods can blow!" 2) To smoke crack in a pipe. 3) To lose something or someone because of one's unwise actions. "He went to basin and shit, blew his ride, his woman, everythang."

BLOW[2]

1) A jazz performance. 2) Cocaine in a powdered form that is SNORTed. Crossover meaning.

BLOW OUT

Natural hair with the tight curls (KINKS) blown out with a

hair dryer to make the hair look full; a popular style in the 1960s and 1970s.

BLOW THE GLASS

To smoke crack in a pipe.

BLOW UP[1]

To suddenly come into a lot of money. "Nigga wudn't nothin befoe. Then he just blew up."

BLOW UP[2]

A natural hairstyle, cut short.

BLUE

The police. Also *blue light special*.

BLUE-EYED DEVIL

A EUROPEAN AMERICAN; less often, but also, a European. Also *devil*.

BLUE-EYED SOUL

A reference to the existence of deep feeling, high emotion, intense spirituality—SOUL—in European Americans and Europeans. Also *blue-eyed soul Sista/Brotha*.

BLUE-EYED SOUL SISTA / BROTHA

See BLUE-EYED SOUL.

BLUE LIGHT SPECIAL

1) A cheap, low-quality brand of clothing, furniture, or other item. 2) See BLUE.

BLUES

1) A feeling of depression, often resulting from a love relationship that's not going right. 2) A reference to a person who is incarcerated; derived from a description of the type of clothes that person is now wearing, the typical drab blue prison uniform. "He's wearing the blues these days."

BLUNT

Marijuana rolled in cigar paper, creating a big marijuana cigarette that has the look of a cigar. See also PHILLY BLUNT.

BMT

Black man talking; used to reinforce a statement. "Lissen up! This is a BMT." Stated in an aggressive, authoritative tone from somebody who obviously knows what he's talking about, the statement reflects a healthy injection of ego. However, used in the presence of women, it may be viewed as asserting authority based strictly on maleness, rather than knowledge, and thus perceived as a chauvinistic statement.

BMW

Black man working. The abbreviation and the expression SIGNIFY ON racism and the economic discrimination that result in overwhelming numbers of African American men being unemployed; thus, one working is a valuable luxury, like the BMW automobile, and a rarity because he has beaten the odds of a system arrayed against him.

BNIC

Boss Nigger in Charge. See HNIC.

BODACIOUS

Bold; superb; outrageously HIP. Crossover term.

BO-DICK

See BO-JACK.

BODY BAG

A condom.

BODY SHOP

A hospital; a place for "fixing" the body.

BOGARD (PRONOUNCED BO-GOD)

To aggressively take over or take charge of something. From film star Humphrey *Bogart*, who played strong-arm tough guys. Older term resurfacing in HIP HOP: "I don't ask, the Ice jes bogard" (from Rapper Ice-T's 1988 *Power* album).

BOGUE

Derogatory, negative, not good. From Hausa *boko*, literally, "deceit" or "fake."

BO-JACK

A form of address for any male. "Bo-jack, my man, whassup?" Also *Bo-dick, Jack.*

BO-JACK

See BOZACK (newer term).

THE BOMB

1) The height of something; the ultimate quality of anything. 2) An outstanding grade of marijuana.

BONE[1]

1) A marijuana cigarette. 2) The penis. 3) A dollar bill. 4) A skinny person, usually female; a negative term. "You better start eatin, girl. Don't nobody want no bone."

BONE[2]

To perform sex, from the male viewpoint. Probably a resurfacing of and variation on *love bone* (older term).

BONE OUT

To leave.

BONED OUT

1) Without money. 2) Describes a man who has just completed sex with a woman.

BONES

Dominoes.

BOO

Marijuana. Crossover term.

BOO-BOO

Euphemism for *shit.*

BOO-COOS

A lot of something; very much; many. From AAE pronunciation of French *beaucoup*. Probably came into Black Talk from soldiers fighting in Europe during the two World

Wars. The French were reported to have been very friendly and receptive to African American soldiers.

BOODY¹

See BACK. For emphasis and dramatic effect, may be pronounced "boo-tay." See also GIT SOME BOODY.

BOODY²

1) Weak. 2) Gullible.

BOODY GREEN

A dance performed by moving the hips suggestively while bending the knees; popular in the 1950s and 1960s. Also *Boody Queen.* The dance resurfaced in the 1980s as *the Butt,* performed in Spike Lee's film *School Daze.*

BOODY QUEEN

See BOODY GREEN.

BOOGIE¹

Any kind of dance step or dance event; originally from *boogie-woogie,* a form of dancing popular in the 1930s.

BOOGIE²

To party, have a good time. Crossover term.

BOOGIE DOWN

To party.

BOOGIE-WOOGIE

See BOOGIE.

BOOGUH-BEAR

See BEAR.

BOOJEE

1) An elitist, uppity-acting African American, generally with a higher educational and income level than the average Black, who identifies with European American culture and distances him/herself from other African Americans. Derived from "bourgeois/bourgeoisie." 2) Describes a person, event, style, or thing that is characteristic of elitist, uppity-acting Blacks. "It was one of them ol boojee thangs."

BOOK¹

In BID, the four cards played each round. See also SET BOOK, TURN A BOOK.

BOOK²

1) To leave. 2) To study (older usage). Both meanings have crossed over.

BOOM

A widely used filler, with no particular meaning. "First, I'm gon finish college, then, boom, I'm a git a good job. Boom. Git a dope ride. Git that crib. Hook it up like I want. Boom. I'm gon be livin large."

BOOM BOX

A large portable stereo. Carried around, usually by males, on a routine basis. Crossover term.

BOOMIN¹

Good-looking.

BOOMIN²

Playing loud and deep bass tones on one's stereo or BOOM BOX.

BOONES

Boone's Farm, a brand of cheap wine.

BOOSTER

A person whose principal source of income is derived from shoplifting and then selling the stolen goods. Older term that has crossed over.

BOOT

An African American. The term is used neutrally, but may come from a source with rather negative associations, boot-black.

BOOT UP

1) To get ready to fight. 2) To put on a condom.

BOP¹

1) A dance with a partner, executed with intricate steps,

twirls, and turns; dates from the 1950s, but still current in many circles. 2) A form of jazz combining African and European rhythms, associated with the music of Charlie Parker, Dizzy Gillespie, and Thelonious Monk; a variation of the term BE-BOP.

BOP²

To walk in a certain rhythmic, graceful, cool way. "He was just boppin down the street." Crossover meaning.

BORN AGAIN

Refers to a person who has been rescued (SAVED) from the world of sin and transformed to a different level of existence.

BOSS

Older term that has crossed over. See DEF (newer term).

BOSS LIKE HOT SAUCE

SuperBOSS; excellent, superb, more boss than boss.

BOSTON

In the game of BID, to win every round of play, to turn all the books (see TURN A BOOK). Also *run a Boston*.

BOTTOM

An area of any city or town where African Americans live. Also *bottoms*. Over time this has come to refer to a rundown or slum area in the Black community. See also BLACK BOTTOM.

BOTTOMS

See BOTTOM.

BOURGEOIS / BOURGEOISIE

See BOOJEE.

BOUT

See BE BOUT.

BOX

1) See BRICK. 2) A stereo. Crossover meaning.

BOY

1) Used to refer to, but not to address, one's male friend or

associate. "Me and my boys was chillin." *Boy* should never be used to address any Black male over eight or nine years old; considered insulting. 2) Any male that one admires or identifies with, whether personally known to one or not; used with *my, your, his,* etc. "Ice Cube gave Project 2000 nem some money for they program? All right! Now, that's my boy." 3) Heroin; older meaning that has crossed over.

BOYFRIEND
A form of address for, or reference to, any male; used primarily by females.

BOZACK
Penis. Also *bo-jack* (older term).

BRA STRAP
To be "on a woman's *bra strap*" is to impose oneself on her, to be bothering or hassling her. For the male version of this, see JOCK STRAP.

BREAK
1) To run or get away. 2) In basketball (and occasionally also football), to FAKE OUT the defense and create scoring opportunities in such a way as to break the defender's spirit and embarrass him/her.

BREAK DOWN
To go low to the floor while dancing.

BREAK IT DOWN
To explain something; to simplify a thing. Also *run it down.*

BREAK ON SOMEBODY
1) To talk negatively about somebody. 2) To embarrass a person in front of others.

BREAK OUT
1) To leave. 2) To bring something out of the place where it has been stored or kept. "In a couple of weeks, when I lose this weight, Ima break out the red dress."

BREAK SOMEBODY'S FACE
 To hurt someone's feelings.

BREAK WIDE
 To leave in a hurry.

BREAKDOWN
 A shotgun.

BREW
 Beer. Crossover term.

BRICK
 1) A woman with a sexy, attractive shape, especially if she has BACK. "She's built like a brick"; "She's a brick." Also *brick house, box.* 2) In basketball, a hard shot that misses the basket and hits the backboard or rim with an ugly sound. See also THROW UP A BRICK.

BRICK HOUSE
 See BRICK.

BRIGHT
 Describes a light-complexioned (HIGH YELLUH) Black person; used without the ambivalent meanings associated with YELLUH and *high yelluh.*

BRING / BRANG THE NOISE!
 Turn on and/or up the music; Git loud and LIVE; Let's PAR-TAY. Also *Pump up the volume!, Pump it up!*

BROAD
 A generic term for a woman, used by women as well as men. Generally not derogatory.

BROKE DOWN
 Describes a stylish way of wearing a hat (usually by a male), such as cocked to one side or tilted forward.

BROTHA
 Any African American male. Derived from the Traditional Black Church pattern of referring to all male members of the Church "family" as *Brotha.*

BROWN-SKIN

Refers to an African American whose skin color is between light- and dark-complexioned.

BS

Crossover expression for *bullshit.*

BUCK

A generic term for an African American man; dates back to enslavement; a negative term.

BUCK[1]

1) To shoot at somebody. 2) To take somebody's money.

BUCK[2]

Completely, totally; extremely. "They was buck wild."

BUCK TEETH

Upper middle two front teeth that protrude outward.

BUCK WHYLIN

Engaging in general conversational chitchat; LYIN and SIGNIFYIN in the Black Verbal Tradition. See also SHOOT THE SHIT, SHOOT THE GIFT.

BUCKET

A beat-up car, usually an older model.

BUCKET OF BLOOD

A rowdy, rough place of entertainment—enter at your own risk.

BUD

Marijuana. Crossover term.

BUDDHA GRASS

Marijuana.

BUFFALO SOLDIERS

Black soldiers in the nineteenth century U.S. Cavalry; so named by Native Americans because of the soldiers' bravery, similar to the courage of the buffalo, which the Native Americans revered—hence *buffalo soldier* was a term of high respect. Many went on to become the nation's first

Black cowboys. Mario Van Peebles' 1993 film, *Posse,* portrayed *buffalo soldiers* who fought in the Spanish-American War.

BUFFALO STANCE

The posture taken by the BUFFALO SOLDIERS before attack, positioning themselves for battle. By extension, today *buffalo stance* refers to an aggressive posture, standing in a position ready to fight.

BUG

To get on somebody's nerves; to irritate a person. From the Mandingo language, *baga,* and the Wolof language, *bugal,* "to annoy." Older term that has crossed over. Also *bug out* (newer term).

BUG OUT

1) To have fun; act CRAZY. 2) See BUG (older term). "No matter where I go, my man complains; he bugs me out."

BULLDAGGER

A lesbian; a derogatory term.

BULLET

A one-year prison sentence.

BUM RUSH

To take over something; to aggressively take charge.

THE BUMP

A 1970s dance in which partners bumped in rhythm against each other's lower bodies.

BUMP

To have sex. A resurfacing and extension of the name of the 1970s dance, the BUMP.

BUMP ONE'S GUMS

To talk excessively.

BUMP UP

To play music louder.

BUMPER KIT

See BACK.

BUMPIN
1) High-energy, loud, especially in reference to music. 2) See DEF.

BUMPIN TITTIES
Fighting.

BUN
To have sex.

BUPPIE
Black urban professional. A middle-class, sophisticated African American; one who is into materialism and self-indulgence, rather than DOWN FOR Black causes.

BURN
1) To cook extremely well and produce food of superior quality and taste. 2) To give someone a sexually transmitted disease. 3) To deceive or manipulate someone into doing something not in that person's best interests, particularly in reference to deceiving someone financially. Meanings (2) and (3) have crossed over.

BUS
To have fun, HANG OUT.

BUS A CAP
To shoot a gun. *Bus* is the AAE pronunciation of "bust." Also *pop a cap, peel a cap*.

BUS ON SOMEBODY
To inform on a person doing anything he/she shouldn't be doing, to get the person BUSTED.

BUS ONE'S NUTS
To have an orgasm, generally used in reference to males. See also GIT A NUT.

BUS SOMEBODY
To catch a person red-handed doing something he/she shouldn't be doing.

BUS SOMEBODY OUT
To have sex with someone, from the male viewpoint.

THE BUS STOP

See the HUSTLE.

BUSH

1) Female pubic hair. Crossover meaning. 2) Marijuana.

BUSINESS

See BIDNESS.

BUST A CAP, BUST ON SOMEBODY, etc.

See BUS A CAP, BUS ON SOMEBODY, etc.

BUSTED

Caught doing something one wasn't supposed to be doing, something wrong or against the rules; can involve either being caught directly or being informed on by someone. Sometimes used humorously for small infractions, as in the case of the SISTA who caught her supposedly dieting girlfriend at a Baskin Robbins ice cream store: "Girl, what you doin up here in '31'? Un-huh, girlfriend, you done got busted." See also BUS ON SOMEBODY, BUS SOMEBODY.

BUSTIN OUT

Describes someone who is looking good at the moment, either because the person is well-dressed, or has an attractive hairstyle, or looks physically fit, or any of a variety of reasons.

THE BUTT

See BOODY GREEN.

BUTTER

1) Something nice. 2) Crack cocaine.

BUY A WOLF TICKET

See WOOF.

BUY A WOOF TICKET

See WOOF.

BUZZ

A high from liquor or drugs. Crossover term.

ᑕ

CAESAR

See QUO VADIS.

CAKES

1) The vagina. 2) Cocaine, crack, or heroin.

CALI

California.

CALL MYSELF / YOURSELF / HERSELF / etc.

To consider yourself to be doing something; to intend to do a thing without actually achieving your objective. "Girl, what you call yourself doing?" that is, What do you think you're doing?; and "I call myself having this dinner ready on time," that is, I had every intention of accomplishing that goal, but I didn't.

CALL SOMEBODY OUT

1) To challenge somebody about a certain point or issue. 2) To challenge somebody to a fight.

CALL SOMEBODY OUTA THEY NAME

To insult someone; to talk about a person in a negative way, especially to call the person a name or to hurl an accusation at the person. "She come talkin bout I stole her ring. I don't appreciate nobody callin me outa my name" (i.e., implying that she's a thief).

CAMEO CUT

See FADE[1].

CANDY CANE

Cocaine, in either powdered form or as crack.

CANE

Crack.

CAN'T KILL NOTHIN AND WON'T NOTHIN DIE

Having a hard time, doing bad, especially economically. Often used as a response to WHAT UP? or WHASS HAPNIN?

CAP

To SIGNIFY ON somebody, to DIS a person; can be done either in fun or seriously and thus not necessarily to insult someone.

CARBON COPY

1) A phony, a fake, a WANNABE. 2) A person who looks just like his/her parents (older meaning).

CASE

A person's business, situation, or state of being. See also GIT OFF MY CASE, ON SOMEBODY'S CASE, ON THE CASE.

CAT

1) A new synthetic drug that is potentially explosive; stronger than ICE. 2) The vagina. 3) A generic reference to any male (older meaning).

CAT FACES

Wrinkles in clothes when ironing them.

CAT WALK

See GANGSTA LIMP (newer term).

CATCH YOU LATER

Goodbye. Older expression that has crossed over. Also *Later* (another older term); *outa here, Outtie 5000* (newer terms).

CATTING

See GANGSTA LIMP (newer term).

CAVE

A EUROPEAN AMERICAN, also sometimes a European; a negative term. Derived from the belief that whites led a barbaric existence in caves in Europe during the heyday of ancient African civilization.

CCM

Cold cash money.

CHANGES

1) Problems in one's personal life; unanticipated emotional

experiences. Crossover meaning. 2) In jazz, a departure from the main melody, during which the musician improvises.

CHARLIE
Any white male; a negative term. Also *Mista Charlie, Charles, Chuck.*

CHARLES
See CHARLIE.

CHECK
1) To criticize somebody's behavior to get them to stop doing what they're doing. Also *put somebody in check.* 2) In basketball, to stay very close to (to guard) the defensive player and attempt to prevent that player from shooting or passing the ball.

CHECK A/HIS/HER/ etc. TRAP
1) To monitor the status of a situation or plan; to check on one's business, especially in the underground economy. 2) To visit, spend time with, or check on a man or woman that one is having an affair with. "He went uptown to check his trap" (said in reference to a married man who went to visit his girlfriend).

CHECK IT IN
Used in street robberies and muggings as a demand for the person to surrender his/her coat, money, or whatever object the mugger demands.

CHECK IT/THIS/HIM/HER/ etc. OUT
Pay attention to something or someone; observe this or analyze it. Crossover expression.

CHECK YOSEF
Monitor your words, actions, or behavior. "Yourself" pronounced *yosef* in AAE; see Introduction.

CHECK YOU/CHECK YOU OUT
See you; goodbye. Crossover expression.

CHEESE
Crack cocaine.

CHICKEN EATER
A preacher; a derogatory term. Traditionally the preacher ate Sunday dinner at a church member's house and was given his pick of the chicken, with the children eating last, whatever was left. They expressed their resentment by calling the preacher a *chicken eater.*

CHICKEN SHIT
Small-time; petty; inadequate. Crossover expression.

CHILL
1) To relax, hang out, either in the street or at home. Also *chill out, max* (current terms); *cool out* (older term). 2) To stop doing or saying something. 3) To calm down from a high emotional state. Also *chill out, take a chill pill* (current terms); *cool it* (older term). This meaning has crossed over, especially in the use of *chill out.*

CHILL OUT
See CHILL.

CHILL PAD
See CRIB.

CHILLIN
1) Relaxing, taking it easy, hanging out, either in the street or at home. Also *coolin it* (older term). 2) Relaxed, calm. Also *cool, copasetic* (older terms).

CHINA WHITE
Asian heroin.

CHITLIN CIRCUIT
Small bars, clubs, and other places of entertainment located in the segregated South in the days before Black entertainers had crashed the color bar. Entertainers such as Blues singer B. B. King and comic genius Moms Mabley performed on the *chitlin circuit* for modest fees, generally doing one-nighters or making otherwise rather limited ap-

pearances before moving on, usually by bus or car, to the next stop on the *circuit*.

CHITLINS
> The intestines of the hog; require extensive cleaning and long hours of cooking. Historically discarded by European Americans and eaten only by Blacks; now an expensive delicacy that many Blacks can't afford.

CHI-TOWN (PRONOUNCED SHY-TOWN)
> Chicago. Also *Windy City*.

CHOCOLATE CITY
> Any city with a predominantly African American population. From the JAM "Chocolate City," by popular 1970s popular FUNK group, Parliament-Funkadelic, founded by musical guru George Clinton, who also coined the phrase "Vanilla Suburb" in the same recording. Clinton and P-Funk are now enjoying a revival in RAP as, for instance, in Dr. Dre's "Let Me Ride" video.

CHOKE
> To lose your nerve in the face of pressure; to fail to accomplish something in a high-stakes situation that you are capable of doing or may even have done before. Also *sell out*.

CHOOSE
> To select a partner for love or sex. The person who gets selected is said to have been *chose*.

CHOSE
> See CHOOSE.

CHUCK
> See CHARLIE.

CHUMP CHANGE
> A small amount of money. Also *crumbs*.

CLAIM
> To indicate the gang you belong to.

CLEAN[1]
> 1) Stylishly dressed. Also *laid*. 2) Dressed up, whether in the

current style or not. 3) Free of drug use; older meaning that has crossed over.

CLEAN²

Totally, completely. "I clean forgot the time"; "All the food was clean gone." Crossover meaning.

CLIP

A clip for an automatic or semiautomatic gun.

CLIPPED

See GIT CLIPPED.

CLIQUE

See POSSE.

CLOCK

1) To stare at; to watch. 2) To make a lot of money. 3) To hit someone. 4) To sell drugs.

CLOW

A game played with dice.

CLOWN¹

1) To ridicule, humiliate. Also *house.* 2) To talk or act inappropriately, especially in public; to act up.

CLOWN²

A state of having fun; one's good-time, partying side. "I couldn't get my clown off," that is, I couldn't get my good-timing in motion due to lack of money for the RIDE that would have put me in a position to have fun.

CLUCKHEAD

A person addicted to crack (or other drugs).

COAL

1) Added before a word to indicate that something is being done intensely or strenuously. "We just coal chillin," meaning, We are really relaxing. 2) Used to describe a person who tells it like it is, dares to speak the unvarnished truth, cuts to the chase. Also *coal-blooded.* 3) Describes something done superbly. "The performance was coal." "Cold" is rendered as *coal* in AAE; see Introduction.

COAL-BLOODED
    1) See COAL. 2) Harshly critical; making a severe hard-line judgment about something or someone.

COAL CHILLIN
    See COAL.

COCK
    Vagina.

COCK BLOCK
    See BLOCK.

COCK BLOCKER
    See BLOCK.

COCK DIESEL
    See DIESEL.

COCK STRONG
    See DIESEL.

COCK SUCKER
    A man who is weak, passive, emasculated. Derived from the notion that a man who performs oral sex is a weakling; the myth is that African American men don't GO DOWN ON women.

COCKTAIL
    A marijuana cigarette butt smoked by putting it in the end of a regular cigarette that has had some of the tobacco emptied out. Crossover term.

COLD
    See COAL.

COLD-BLOODED
    See COAL-BLOODED.

COLOM
    Marijuana imported from Colombia. Also *commercial*.

COLOR SCALE
    The gradation of skin color values, from very light-complexioned to very dark-complexioned.

COLOR STRUCK

Denotes an African American obsessed with, and preferring, light-complexioned Blacks; the term is used negatively since it suggests a preference for whiteness.

COLORED

Refers to a person of African descent. The preferred term until about the 1920s; still heard among older Blacks today. See also COLORED PEOPLE, PEOPLE OF COLOR, and Introduction.

COLORED PEOPLE

People of African descent; used primarily by senior Blacks. Also *Colored*. The founders of the NAACP, the oldest Civil Rights organization, used this racial designation when they organized the NAACP in 1909. It has remained the National Association for the Advancement of *Colored People* ever since, despite the shifts from NEGRO to BLACK to AFRICAN AMERICAN. With the emerging prominence of "colored" groups in the population (Latinos/Hispanics, Asians, etc.), this designation may be revived as a generic term for PEOPLE OF COLOR. In fact, the newly appointed national director of the NAACP, the Reverend Dr. Benjamin F. Chavis, Jr., proposes to extend the NAACP to include Hispanics, Asians, and American Indians, who, like African Americans, face discrimination as *Colored People*. See also COLORED, PEOPLE OF COLOR, and Introduction.

COLORED PEOPLE'S TIME

Also *CPT, CP Time*. See AFRICAN PEOPLE'S TIME.

COLORS

Symbolic colors that show one's group affiliation. Used by motorcycle clubs as well as gangs.

COME

Used to express indignation at or disapproval of someone's

. . . .

actions or words. In a conversation between male and female, the SISTA said: "Don't come tellin me bout no late buses and all that; you just late and you messed up."

COME AGAIN

Please repeat what you said because I don't understand you. Crossover expression.

COME BACKED UP

Used by women in reference to a woman who has had sex over an extended period of time but due to her male partner's inadequacy has not achieved orgasm.

COME OUT

Used in reference to losing one's hair, as in "The perm was too strong and my hair come out." Also *fall out*.

COME OUT OF A BAG

To act contrary to expectations; to behave illogically for the situation. "You can try talkin to him, it might help, but ain no tellin, he might come out of a bag."

COME WIT IT

A challenge for a person to produce whatever it is they think they've got that is the very best of something; used in sports, card playing, verbal dueling, fights, and other forms of competition. Also *set it out*.

COMMERCIAL

See COLOM.

COMMUNITY

The African American community.

CONEY ONEY

A Detroit gang; no longer in existence.

CONK

A male hairstyle, popular before the 1970s, in which the hair is STRAIGHTENed using a mixture of lye, white potatoes, and eggs. Also *do, process*. Malcolm X wrote about the experience in his *Autobiography*: "I got a can of Red

Devil lye. . . . 'It's going to burn when I comb it in—it burns *bad*. But the longer you can stand it, the straighter the hair.' . . . I couldn't stand it any longer; I bolted to the washbasin." Later Malcolm says: "This was the trip to Michigan in the wintertime when I put congolene on my head, then discovered that the bathroom sink's pipes were frozen. To keep the lye from burning up my scalp, I had to stick my head into the stool and flush and flush to rinse out the stuff." This scene was reproduced in Spike Lee's film *Malcolm X*.

CONSTANT

A person who is a perennial or habitual part of a scene or situation, usually hanging around to run a scam, e.g., an ex-student on a university campus who plies drugs to current students.

CONVERSATE

To carry on a conversation, usually a lively, colorful one.

CONVERSATION

One's RAP (in the romantic sense); the style of talk one uses to HIT ON a man or woman.

COOCHIE

Euphemism for PUSSY.

COOKIE

Crack in a rock or solid form.

COOKIN

1) Doing something energetically and with skill. Crossover meaning. 2) Playing jazz with intense enthusiasm, fervor, and excellence.

COOKIN WITH GAS

Used as a response of encouragement to a speaker, meaning, You ON THE CASE, that's right, now you talkin.

COOL[1]

1) Relaxed, calm. Also *chillin* (newer term); *copasetic*

(older term). 2) Okay, fine with me. Also *copasetic*. 3) Excellent, great. Also *def*. All three meanings have crossed over.

COOL[2]

Composure, calmness; not displaying one's feelings or reactions. Crossover term.

COOL IT

See CHILL (newer term).

COOL OUT

See CHILL (newer term).

COOLIN IT

See CHILLIN (newer term).

COOLNESS

See COOL[2].

COP

To obtain something. "I copped a new ride, and she didn like it, so I copped a tude."

COP A PLEA

To surrender, compromise; to give in.

COPASETIC

1) Relaxed, calm. Also *cool* (newer term); *chillin* (latest term). 2) Okay, fine with me. Also *cool*. Although used primarily by senior Blacks, *copasetic* may be resurfacing in HIP HOP Culture, as in the line "Everything is copasetic" in the recent JAM "Shu-Be," by the group Guess.

CORN ROWS

Small braids arranged close to the head, using synthetic or human hair "extensions" braided into the natural hair; the style dates back to ancient Africa.

CORNY

Stale, not with-it. Also *wack*.

CO-SIGN

To verify or affirm a statement or action of another.

Derived from the frequent necessity for African Americans to have someone *co-sign* for them before they can obtain credit.

COULDN'T HIT HIM/HER IN THE BEHIND WITH A RED APPLE

Used to refer to: 1) A person who is arrogant or conceited. 2) A know-it-all. 3) A headstrong person.

THE COUNT

The population. Taken from jail life, where it refers to the counting of the inmates periodically performed by guards in order to ascertain if any prisoners are missing. Anybody who gets killed or is otherwise missing is said to have been "taken off *the count*."

COUNTERFEIT

In the game of BID, the BOOK of cards that the player who has the BID discards before the first round of play.

CP TIME

Colored People's Time. See AFRICAN PEOPLE'S TIME.

CPT

Colored People's Time. See AFRICAN PEOPLE'S TIME.

CRABS

An insulting name used by the Los Angeles gang the BLOODS for their former rivals, the CRIPS.

CRACK ON

To DIS a person, either seriously or in fun.

CRACKED OUT

Thoroughly and completely addicted to crack.

CRACKER

A white person; a derogatory term. Possibly derived from the sound of the master's whip during enslavement; by extension, any white person.

CRACKHEAD

A person addicted to crack. Crossover term. Also *smoker, puffer, rock star*.

CRACKIN BUT FACKIN

Making humorous or joking statements that are very factual. "Facting" pronounced *fackin* in AAE; see Introduction.

CRAPPED OUT

1) To have lost out in any big competition, fight, or struggle. 2) To have hit rock bottom.

CRAZY

1) A lot of; very much; a great deal. "He got crazy digits at the party," meaning, He collected a lot of phone numbers and addresses. Also *mad*. 2) Going against conventional behavior for African Americans, particularly against European Americans' conventions and expectations for Blacks; an older, long-standing meaning. "Don't nobody pay no attention to no nigga that ain crazy," meaning, In order to draw attention to your cause or situation, you must go against the norms that whites have set for Blacks. 3) Describes any action that is unconventional or nonconformist, whether racially based or not. 4) Describes a person who is having fun, telling jokes, making everybody laugh by his/her behavior or comments. Also *sick*.

CREEP

1) To sneak out with somebody other than your husband/wife/partner. 2) To stalk somebody maliciously. 3) To ride slowly in a car.

CREW

See POSSE.

CRIB

A house; one's home. Also *den, joint, pad* (older terms); *chill pad* (newer term).

CRIMEY

One's partner; sometimes literally one's partner in crime, but also used to refer to one's close associate, intimate, or partner in a generic sense.

CRIPS

> A gang in Los Angeles. The name is derived from the founder of the *Crips,* who was a member of the Chicago gang the Blackstone Rangers. After being shot and crippled in Chicago, he moved to Los Angeles and founded his own gang, naming it the *Crips.* The *Crips* and their former rivals, the Bloods, have received widespread notice in the last few years; see the discussion at BLOODS.

CRONZ

> A gun.

CROSS OUT

> A gang term referring to the defacing or crossing out of the graffiti of a rival gang.

CROSS OVAH

> See GO OVAH.

CROSS THE BURNING SANDS

> Refers to the initiation ritual of African American fraternities and sororities. See also GO OVAH.

CRUMB SNATCHERS

> Children. Also *rug rats, table pimps.*

CRUMBS

> 1) LOW-LIFE people. 2) Unimportant people, not necessarily low-life. 3) See CHUMP CHANGE.

CRYSTAL

> Cocaine that hasn't been diluted (CUT) with baking powder, quinine, or other fillers; "pure" cocaine.

CURB

> Ugly; undesirable.

A / THE CURL

> Originally referred to the JHERI-CURL; now also used to refer to any of the several spinoff imitations of the Jheri.

CUT

> 1) To put a person in his/her place; to verbally set someone

straight; tell someone off. "If she say one more thang to me, Ima cut her every which way but loose." 2) To dilute the strength or purity of anything (not just drugs). "When you makin this kind of pie, you got to cut the lemon with a lot of sugar." 3) To injure a person by using a razor or knife. "My partners got cut bad in that fight."

CUT SOMEBODY SOME SLACK

To ease up the pressure; give somebody a break. Also *give somebody some slack, slack.*

CUZ

A form of address (and reference) to your HOMEY.

D

D

Detroit. Also *Big D,* which has not crossed over; *Motor City* and *Motown,* which have crossed over.

D

1) Defense in basketball. 2) By extension, defensive posture and moves in general. 3) Euphemism for *dick* (penis).

D-UP

1) To tighten up the defense in basketball. 2) By extension, to intensify your defensive mode in any area of your life where you are vulnerable.

D-WHUPPED

See DICK-WHUPPED.

DAISY DUKES

See DAZZEY DUKS.

THE DAP

A style of handshake executed with elaborate movements;

very popular among Blacks during the Vietnam War and today among Vietnam veterans.

DAP

Stylishly dressed.

DARK-SKIN

Refers to a dark-complexioned African American.

A DAY LATE AND A DOLLAR SHORT

Unprepared, disorganized, unready; having failed to live up
to one's commitments.

DAY ONE

The first day something started; the beginning. "I been doin
it this way since Day One [the first day of the speaker's em-
ployment], and now he come tellin me I ain doin it right."

DAZZEY DUKS

Very tight, scanty female shorts that reveal the flesh of the
lower buttocks. Derived from the name of the female character Daisy Duke, who wore such shorts in the early 1980s
television sitcom "The Dukes of Hazzard." Resurfacing in
HIP HOP, as in the popular 1993 JAM "Dazzey Duks" by
Rapper Duice.

DBI SYNDROME

Declaration of Black Inferiority; used in reference to Blacks
with low self-esteem who have taken on society's racism
and feel that African Americans are inferior to European
Americans.

D.C.

Washington, D.C.

DEAD

1) Used in the Traditional Black Church to refer to the absence of spirit, emotion, enthusiasm. In the Traditional
Black Church, the motto is "If you got religion, you
oughtta show some sign." 2) By extension, used in the
world outside the Church to describe an absence of spirit or

feeling in any situation. 3) Describes a situation, person, or event that has been put to rest or forgotten; out of style.

DEAD CAT ON THE LINE
Something suspicious.

DEAD PRESIDENTS
Money. A reference to the pictures of U.S. Presidents on dollar bills.

DEAD RAG
A dead gang member. From the style of wearing a scarf or handkerchief around the head to identify one's gang affiliation.

THE DEAL
The actual situation or state of things; how things stand at a particular point in time. Older crossover term resurfacing in HIP HOP, as in Public Enemy's "Black Steel in the Hour of Chaos," on their 1988 album, *It Takes A Nation of Millions To Hold Us Back.*

DEALIN
See ROLLIN (newer term).

DECOY
A fake drug; a mixture sold as crack or cocaine that is nothing but a mishmash of baby powder, quinine, baking soda, and other fillers. Also GANKER.

DEEP
Serious; describes a person, thing, or event that has a powerful or profound meaning.

DEF
Great; superb; excellent. Derived from an older expression, DO IT TO DEF, using the AAE pronunciation of "death"; see Introduction. *Doin it to def* means doing something excellently, superbly—DOIN IT TO THE MAX. Also *boss, mean, cool, hip, terrible, outa sight, monsta, dynamite*

(older terms); *fresh, hype, jammin, slammin, kickin, bumpin, humpin, phat, pumpin, stoopid stupid, vicious, down, dope, on, raw* (newer terms).

DELIVER

To perform something to the maximum. "The concert was hype; my girls, Boss [a hot new female RAP group], shonuff delivered."

DEN

See CRIB.

DEUCE-AND-A-QUARTER

A Buick automobile, the Electra 225 model; once a very popular status symbol.

DEUCE-FIVE

A .25-caliber handgun.

DEVIL

1) Any white person, equating whites with the sinister, immoral, and corrupt character of Satan. From the Nation of Islam's (see The NATION) founding tenet about the introduction of evil into ancient Black paradise through the unwise creation of YACUB, a scientist whose inventive curiosity went too far and produced a monstrous *devil*, the white man. In recent years, under the leadership of Minister Louis Farrakhan, The Nation has moderated its position in this regard. 2) In the vocabulary of the FIVE PERCENT NATION, which was established by former members of the Nation of Islam in 1964, *devil* was extended to include any person who, like the "Caucasian white man," is immoral, corrupt, sinister, and evil.

DIASPORA

A generic reference to the various geographical areas outside of Africa where Africans were enslaved, principally North, South, and Central America and the Caribbean, i.e., the so-called "New World."

DICHTY

Uppity-acting, putting on airs; haughty, arrogant. Also *sa-diddy* (newer term).

DICK-WHUPPED

Refers to a woman who is so in love that she lets her MAN rule her and boss her around; describes a woman victimized by sexual desire. Also *d-whupped*. Males in a similar situation are said to be PUSSY-WHUPPED.

DIE

See SHOOT THE DIE.

DIESEL

Describes a muscular, large-sized build. Also *cock diesel, cock strong; thick* (older term).

DIG

1) To understand, comprehend. Crossover meaning. 2) To like or love a person, event, or idea. "I don't dig nobody messin wit my feelings." From Wolof *dega*, "to understand."

DIG ON

To observe or pay attention to something.

DIGITS

1) A person's phone number and/or address. 2) The amount of a check, usually a paycheck. A resurfacing and extension of the term *digits*, meaning a set of numbers, used in the heyday of the NUMBER GAME to refer to a number that fell (see FALL) or was played.

DIME

1) Ten dollars. 2) Ten years; often used in reference to a prison sentence. 3) A quantity of marijuana selling for ten dollars (a *dime* BAG). Crossover meaning.

DIPPIN

Being nosy; sticking your nose into or getting involved in another person's business or conversation.

DIS¹

To discount or show disrespect for a person; to put someone down. Sometimes done in a ritual of verbal play, and thus not always to be taken seriously.

DIS²

1) In BID, the cards that are discarded by the bidder before play begins. 2) An expression of disrespect; an instance of DISsin.

DIVA

1) A stately, grand woman, a "trophy," who may or may not be a beauty. 2) A female Rapper or other musical entertainer who is superbly talented. 3) By extension, any accomplished woman in any walk of life.

DJ

1) A technician who accompanies the Rapper in RAP Music. 2) A disc jockey in the traditional sense, who selects and plays music for an audience, either live or on the radio.

DL

Refers to something done sneakily, on the sly, literally, "down low."

DO¹

1) To have sexual intercourse with someone. 2) To perform oral sex on someone. 3) To beat up or kill someone.

DO²

See CONK.

DO A BID

To serve time in prison.

DO A BIG

To commit a robbery.

DO A GHOST

To leave.

DO-DO

Pronounced like the verb "do." Nothing; something unimportant. "What he was talkin bout didn mean do-do to me."

DO-IT FLUID
Liquor, usually gin, believed to increase a male's sexual stamina and potency.

DO IT TO DEF
See DEF.

DO IT TO THE MAX
1) To do something intensely, vigorously, strenuously. 2) To do something to the height of excellence.

DO ONE'S OWN / YO THANG
To behave, perform, or do something in your own unique way, according to your own individual style; used in reference to an activity, wearing a certain hairstyle or style of clothes, playing a certain role in a group, your own unique contribution to something, your creation or idea. From Mandingo *ka a fen ke,* literally, "to do one's thing." Also simply *yo Thang,* as in "Las Vegas? Not the Kid; that's yo Thang" (said by a SISTA to her husband, indicating that she does not wish to go to Las Vegas, because gambling is not her style but his).

DO-RAG
1) A scarf, handkerchief, or STOCKING CAP worn by a male to keep his hair in place and preserve his DO. The term originated in the era when do's/PROCESSes/CONKS were stylish. See also HEAD RAG. 2) Among gangs, a scarf or handkerchief worn around the head to identify gang affiliation.

DODGERS
Cockroaches.

DOG¹
1) A form of address and greeting used mainly, but no longer exclusively, for males. Most likely from the African

American fraternity tradition of referring to members and pledges as *dogs;* for example, an Alpha *dog* is a member of Alpha Phi Alpha fraternity. Although a symbol of male bonding, "Yo, Dog!" was misunderstood by a European American male psychiatrist treating an incarcerated African American male. The psychiatrist thought the BROTHA was insulting him by calling him a "dog" and ordered the Brotha confined. 2) A promiscuous man; a man who, according to some women, "will fuck anythang." 3) An ugly female; older meaning that has crossed over.

DOG²

1) To mistreat someone. 2) To insult someone; to criticize or talk about a person negatively. Also *dog somebody out.*

DOG SOMEBODY OUT

See DOG².

DOGS

1) Gym shoes. 2) Feet; older meaning that has crossed over.

DOME

Head.

DOME PIECE

A hat.

DON'T DEAL IN COAL

Does not date or engage in romance with any dark-complexioned African American.

DON'T MAKE ME NONE

It makes no difference to me; it's irrelevant to me.

DOOBIE

A marijuana cigarette, or marijuana itself. Term in process of crossing over.

DOODLY-SQUAT

Nothing; or if it is something, it's something worthless. Probably a euphemism for *shit.* "Them forms ain't worth doodly-squat to me, I ain't fillin out nothin." Crossover term.

DOOFUS

A person or thing that is out of touch with the times, un-HIP; also someone or something that is sloppy or disorganized. "This is the most doofus meeting I've ever been to, what a waste of time!"

DOO-WAH-DIDDY

See DOODLY-SQUAT, crossover term. *Doo-wah-diddy,* however, has not crossed over.

DOO-WOP

A style of singing done with a backup group rendering a refrain or background that sounds roughly like "doo-wop" or "doo-wah"; popular in the 1950s and particularly during the MOTOWN era of the 1960s and 1970s. Resurfacing in some musical groups of today, such as Boyz II Men.

DOPE

1) See DEF. 2) Marijuana, crack, or any other illegal drug.

DOPE FIEND MOVE

A wild or bizarre action; an unexpected move of desperation to accomplish a goal.

DOUBLE DEUCE

A .22-caliber handgun.

DOUBLE DUTCH

A game of jump rope, played by females, in which players have to jump over two ropes instead of one, as the ropes are turned around and over each other in an "eggbeater motion," alternating between slow and super-fast speeds, depending on the inclination of the players turning the ropes for the jumpers. The double rope style is believed to have been brought by the Dutch when they settled in "New Amsterdam" (New York)—hence the name *Double Dutch.* The game reflects the Africanized character of other Black children's games, for instance, using rhymed chants to accompany the jumping of the ropes. *Double Dutch,* like B-BALL, became popular in urban HOODS because it could be played anywhere and did not require expensive equipment. The *Double Dutch* tradition originally began as a boys' game, but the SISTAS took it over in the twentieth century, and it has become a training ground for developing rhythm, coordination, and style. A highly competitive game testing dexterity, concentration, and the ability to maintain one's COOL, *Double Dutch* is the Sistas' b-ball. According to the American Double Dutch League (founded in New York City in 1974), the game requires "sharp reflexes, precise motor skills, and an analytic acumen that enables space-time coordination among players. Its styles, themes, and group practices embody cultural symbols useful in exploring and negotiating adolescent identity." In June of 1993, the Annual Double Dutch Tournament was held at Columbia University in New York, taking the Sistas' game right on outside the hood. That tournament not only drew contestants—fourth to eighth graders—from all over the United States, but also a couple of teams from outside the country. The American Double Dutch League is preparing to make *Double Dutch* a part of the Olympics by the year 2000.

DOUBLE-UPS

Refers to the act of buying crack on the basis of two quantities, usually small, for the price of one.

DOWN

1) Agreeable to something; ready to do something; WIT THE PROGRAM, whatever it is. "We gittin ready to make this move. You down"? 2) See DEF. "The concert was down."

DOWN BY LAW

1) Used to describe an expert or experienced professional in his/her work, occupation, or GAME, whatever it is. 2) By extension, describes somebody with high status or anything that's superb.

DOWN FOR

1) Loyal to someone. 2) In favor of or agreeable to a plan or program. "The Sistas was down for the boycott."

DOWN FOR MINE

Able to protect oneself.

DOWN HOME

See HOME.

DOWN LOW

See DL.

DOWN PAT

Mastered or learned perfectly, as a routine, a game, a system, or a technique of doing something. Crossover expression.

DOWN SOUTH

Any place south of the Mason-Dixon Line, once considered the most racist part of the United States. However, Malcolm X coined the expression *up South,* to SIGNIFY ON the mythical notion, held by Blacks for over a hundred years after Emancipation, that the U.S. North was free of segregation and racism.

DOWN WITH

1) Part of a group. 2) Supporting or endorsing a group or a program.

DOWN WITH THE NATION

1) Refers to a member of the Nation of Islam, led by Minister Louis Farrakhan. See The NATION. 2) Refers to anybody who supports or endorses the Nation of Islam.

THE DOZENS

A verbal ritual of talking negatively about someone's mother (or occasionally grandmothers and other female relatives) by coming up with outlandish, highly exaggerated, often sexually loaded, humorous "insults"; played among friends, associates, and those HIP to the game. The objective is to outtalk one's competitor, get the most laughs from the group, and not lose emotional control. A fundamental rule is that the "slander" must not be literally true because truth takes the group out of the realm of play into reality. Although females also *play the dozens,* the game's usual players are males, who use it to test not only their verbal skills but also their capacity to maintain their COOL. The term, though not the ritual itself, is believed to have originated during enslavement, wherein slave auctioneers sold defective "merchandise," e.g., sick slaves or older slaves, in lots of a dozen; thus a slave who was part of a dozens group was "inferior." Portrayed in the 1992 film *White Men Can't Jump.*

DR. THOMAS

See TOM.

DRAG[1]

To con someone. Also *run a drag on.*

DRAG[2]

A person who is a damper on the fun, a party, or other activity. "What's wrong with you? You sho is a drag."

DRAPED

Describes a person wearing a lot of gold jewelry.

DREADLOCKS

A natural hairstyle created by growing one's hair without combing it for several weeks or months; instead, the hair is twisted, and beeswax, coconut oil, and peanut oil are applied; the hair naturally develops into *locks,* loose, thick braids. Popularized by RASTAFARIAN musicians from the Caribbean, perhaps the most well-known being the late Bob Marley, *dreadlocks* epitomized Black rejection of Western society and what journalist Kenneth M. Jones called "a different kind of cool . . . the walk of Black spirits reaching back to Africa" (*Essence,* October 1985). Worn by Rappers and other Blacks (both in and outside of HIP HOP Cul-

ture), *dreadlocks* have gained popularity beyond the RAS-
TAS. Also *dreads*. See also RASTAFARIA.

DREADS
See DREADLOCKS.

DREAM BOOK
A book listing common dreams, names, events, and the
numbers symbolizing these things; consulted by those who
PLAY THE NUMBERS and/or the lottery in the belief that
a dream represents good fortune if one can only interpret it
accurately in order to get the lucky number that will be the
winner. One very popular dream book during the heyday of
the NUMBERS, and one still in use today by those who play
the new state-controlled lotteries, is *The Three Wise Men*.

DRIVE-BY
Shooting done from a vehicle whose occupants shoot at
someone on the street, often in disregard of innocent by-
standers, and then drive on. "They call me 'Lucky' cause I
been in five drive-bys and still here" (from the 1992 film
Trespass).

DROP
To enlighten; to inform; to explain. "Let me drop some science," that is, I'll explain the facts to you.

DROP A DIME
To tell on somebody who is doing something wrong or illegal by reporting that person's activities to somebody who
has power over the person. "We use to go over there all the
time—fuck school—until one day somebody dropped a
dime on us, and the counselor [the school counselor, to
whom the informant talked] told my momma—and the
shit hit the fan." *Dime* can be *dropped* to any authority
figure—the police, a government agency (such as the IRS),
a welfare office, a parent, or a school official. From the time
when telephone calls cost a dime.

DROP A LINE

1) To initiate a conversation or otherwise indicate interest in developing a relationship with someone. 2) To call someone on the telephone.

DROP A LUG

To CAP or SIGNIFY ON somebody; to DIS a person, either seriously or in fun.

DROP IT

Used as a signal to begin, to start something.

DROP TOP

A car with a fabric top that can be lowered; a convertible. Older term that is resurfacing. "I gotta go cause I got me a drop top,/and if I hit the switch, I can make the ass drop" (i.e., activate the LIFTS switch, thus raising the front end of the car and lowering the rear end), from Ice Cube's "It Was A Good Day," on his 1992 album *The Predator.*

DROPPIN BABIES

Having a lot of children.

DUCKETTES

Money.

DUDE

A generic reference to any male. Used to refer to males but not as a form of address, thus: "Ain't none of these dudes bad enough to beat me," but *not* "Hey dude, how you doin?"

DUES

The rough spots in life, hardships; hard times, owed as the debt for the good times. See also PAY DUES.

DUKE

To fight.

DUKIE

Euphemism for SHIT.

DUNK

1) In basketball, to drop the ball into the basket from a po-

sition above the rim. 2) By extension, to outdo or beat opponents or rivals by not playing by the usual rules, allowing them the chance to "block" your "shots," but instead pulling an aggressive surprise move "over their heads." A businessman lost a deal to a competitor, who used an unexpected, unusual business tactic to win the deal: "What can I say? Johnson beat me out, just dunked on me." See also SLAM-DUNK.

DUST

To add the drug PCP to marijuana.

DUSTED

1) High on the drug PCP. See also ANGEL DUST. 2) Outlandish or outrageous.

DYNAMITE

Crossover term. See DEF, newer term that has not crossed over.

E

EAGLE-FLYIN DAY

Payday. From the symbol of the eagle on some U.S. currency.

EARTH

A woman, in the vocabulary of the FIVE PERCENT NATION.

EARTHLY THINGS

A Traditional Black Church term referring to things you can see or feel.

EAT CHEESE

To have oral sex with a woman.

EDGES

The hairline, the first part to GO BACK after hair has been STRAIGHTENed.

EDUCATED FOOL
A person with formal, "book" education, but no common sense, no MOTHER WIT.

EIGHT BALL
Olde English 800 malt liquor.

EIGHT BALL
1) Cocaine and speed mixed together. 2) One-eighth of an ounce of cocaine.

EIGHT ROCK
A very dark-complexioned African American.

EIGHT TRACK
Two and a half grams of cocaine.

EL PEE
An El Producto brand cigar, used to roll a BLUNT.

ELDERS
1) Older men, usually leaders, in the Traditional Black Church. 2) By extension, politically and spiritually developed, wise men and women, not only people older in age.

THE ELECTRIC SLIDE
See the HUSTLE.

E-LIGHT
1) An uppity-acting, elitist African American, usually well-educated and materially well-off, who looks down on less fortunate African Americans. 2) A European American–thinking Black who doesn't identify with the race or Black causes. Probably from AAE pronunciation of "elite," regularizing it to the pronunciation pattern of words like HO-tel, PO-lice, etc.

ENDS
See N's.

ESSEYS
HOMEYS of Hispanic/Latino descent. Derived from the

popular greeting in Chicano Spanish, "Esé," loosely meaning, "Hey, man."

EUROPEAN AMERICAN

An emerging term to replace "white American"; more precise in indicating the land of origin of the "white race," just as AFRICAN AMERICAN indicates the land of origin of Blacks. It brings the term for whites in line with racial labels for other groups in the United States, and is viewed as a healthy move away from the connotations of racial supremacy associated with the designation "white."

EUROPEAN NEGRO

An African American who thinks like and identifies with European Americans, and who rejects Black causes and the Black community. Also *Afro-Saxon* (older term).

EVERYTHANG IS EVERYTHANG

Things are all right; everything is OKAY in the world; suggests the connectedness or oneness of everything.

EVIL

Negative in disposition; mean-spirited; describes a person with a bad—meaning "not good"—TUDE. "Can't nobody say nothin to him; he is one evil ol man."

mission of the artist, Craig Rex Perry, and *Young Sisters and Brothers Magazine.*

EVIL EYE

A certain way of looking at a person to exhibit disapproval or anger. Stems from the belief that a person's eye has the power to bring bad luck or destruction upon somebody.

F

Euphemism for FUCK.

F-IN

Euphemism for FUCKin.

FADE[1]

A male hairstyle, high on top and very short or completely shaved on the sides and back; the top can be NATURAL or dreaded (see DREADLOCKS). Also *cameo cut, high top fade.*

FADE[2]

To cause problems for somebody; generally used in the negative. "Don't fade me."

FADED

1) Out of style. 2) Old. 3) Overused. 4) Drunk.

FAIR

Used to describe an African American with a light skin color. Also *fair-skin, bright, yelluh, high yelluh, light-skin.*

FAIR-SKIN

See *fair.*

FAKE OUT

In basketball, to throw one's opponent off by pretending to make one move while actually making another.

FALL

Used in reference to the number that wins for the day (see NUMBERS). Also *fall out.*

FALL OUT

1) Used not only in reference to disagreement with a person, but also to dissatisfaction or severance of a relationship. "I'm gon fall all the way out with High-Tech Appliance if they don't stop raising they prices every other month." 2) To faint. 3) Used in reference to losing one's hair, not only from the natural process of getting bald, but also from a PERM or other unnatural event or condition, such as mental stress. Also *come out.* 4) Used in reference to the number that wins for the day (see NUMBERS). "Girl, don't you know I should be whupped, my name fell out today," that is, The combination of numbers for the speaker's name, as given in the DREAM BOOK, was the winning number for the day, but she didn't play it. Also *fall.*

FAMILIAR

Acting outside acceptable social boundaries so as to suggest that you are on personal, intimate terms with somebody when, in fact, you are not. Often used to criticize inappropriate behavior toward the opposite sex. "One thang I don't like bout him, he act too familiar for me."

FASS

Describes a female who is acting grown-up (WOMLISH), especially in a sexual manner. The AAE pronunciation of "fast"; see Introduction.

FAT

See *phat.*

FAT MAN AGAINST THE HOLE IN A DOUGHNUT

Used to express certainty about one's prediction or argument; indicates a willingness to risk everything against nothing on the accuracy of one's point. During the 1993 NBA championship series, which featured the Chicago Bulls vs. the Phoenix Suns, the BROTHA said, "I bet you a fat man against the hole in a doughnut the Suns can't come back against Chicago."

FAT MOUTH

1) To talk too much, especially about something you can't back up with facts. 2) To make wild, outlandish threats that you don't have the power or guts to execute. "Dat nigga don't want no action. He just fat mouthin." The term MURDER MOUTH is also used with this meaning. From Mandingo *da-ba*, "excessive talking," literally, "big, fat mouth." *Fat mouth* has crossed over, but MURDER MOUTH has not.

FAY

See OFAY.

FEDERATED

Wearing excessive red, the color of the Los Angeles gang the BLOODS; used by their former rivals, the CRIPS, as a DIS.

FEED SOMEBODY THE PILL

In basketball, to pass the ball to somebody.

FELL OFF

To have lost a lot of weight. "She done really fell off, and she don't look right."

FESS

1) To fake something; to pretend to be something you're not. 2) To promise to do something that you aren't really going to do.

FIELD NIGGA

An African American in the working class, or un-working class, i.e., Blacks laid off, unable to find work, or otherwise unemployed. Historically, an enslaved African who worked in the fields, as opposed to the HOUSE NIGGA, an enslaved African who worked in Ole Massa's household. The *field nigga* was believed to be more predisposed toward rebellion against enslavement than the HOUSE NIGGA, who was viewed as loyal to Massa. The historical roles

were updated in the 1960s by Malcolm X, who asserted
that those Blacks who were working-class, unemployed,
and outside the system—*field niggas*—were likely to reject
and rise up against racism and the system, since they were
in it but not of it, whereas the African American middle and
professional classes—HOUSE NIGGAS—were more likely
to deny the existence of racism or make excuses for it, to
identify with whites and the system, and thus unlikely to
engage in protest or REBELLION.

FIEND
A person with a drug problem.

FIFTY-ONE
A cigarette that is part marijuana and part crack cocaine.
Also *primo, roulie, sleef, spleefer.*

FIGURE
The winning number for the day in the NUMBER GAME or
the lottery.

FINE
Good-looking; used for males or females.

FINESSE[1]
To smooth over something that has the potential for conflict or trouble; to use diplomacy in a SLICK way.

FINESSE[2]
Diplomacy; a type of SLICKness.

FIRE IT UP
To light a marijuana cigarette.

FIRST MIND
The initial idea or thought that a person has about something, believed to be the best course of action because *first
mind* ideas come from intuition and natural instinct, untainted by the conscious mind. "If I had followed my first
mind and played the dead role, I'd be rich now," meaning,
If the speaker had played the number that symbolizes

death, she would have HIT THE NUMBER for a large sum of money.

FISH

The vagina.

FIVE

A slapping of palms to show affirmation, strong agreement, celebration of victory; also used as a greeting. Derived from a West African communication style, as in Mandingo *i golo don m bolo,* literally, "put your skin in my hand," a phrase used to accompany another phrase or statement requesting the listener's show of affirmation. African American women's *five* involves sliding one's forefinger across the forefinger of the other SISTA; for the HIGH FIVE, touching forefingers with the hands held high. See also FIVE ON THE BLACK-HAND SIDE, FIVE ON THE SLY, HIGH FIVE, LOW FIVE, GIVE SOMEBODY FIVE, GIVE SOMEBODY SOME SKIN.

FIVE AND DIME

Poorly dressed; showing bad taste in clothes.

FIVE HUNDRED

See BEAMER.

FIVE-O (pronounced five-OH)

The police; probably derived from the television show "Hawaii Five-O." Also *The Man,* older term that has crossed over.

FIVE ON THE BLACK-HAND SIDE

A FIVE on the outer side of the hand rather than the palm side, that is, on the darker, "Black-hand" side.

FIVE ON THE SLY

A FIVE with the hands held behind the back, down low, done surreptitiously to assert camaraderie without the awareness of onlookers.

FIVE PERCENT NATION

A group established by former members of the Nation of Is-

lam (see The NATION) in 1964 under the leadership of
Clarence "Pudding" 13X. The name derives from the belief
that only five percent of humanity live a proper life, in ac-
cord with the "true divine nature of the Black man who is
God or Allah," and that only those five percent will one day
reign supreme. Also known now as "The Nation of Gods
and Earths," the *Five Percenters* have had a significant impact on youth. According to Professor Yusuf Nuruddin, of
Medgar Evers College in New York: "The influence of the
Five Percent Nation . . . has grown enormously. . . . [They
have produced] offshoot or cognate groups that espouse a
similar ideology; one such group is the Zulu Nation in the
South Bronx. . . . Many of the lyrics in contemporary Rap
Music make direct reference or strong allusion to Five Per-
center ideology" (from "The Five Percenters: A Teenage
Nation of Gods and Earths," in *Muslim Communities in
North America,* edited by Yvonne Yazbeck Haddad and
Jane Idleman Smith, State University of New York Press at
Albany, 1994).

FLAKEY
Unreliable, shaky.

FLAT TOP
A hairstyle with a high, square, flat top; generally, but not
exclusively, male. Similar to a FADE, but a fade can also be
dreaded (see DREADLOCKS) on top.

FLAVOR
1) Attractiveness. 2) Style.

FLEX
To try to impress people by showing off; used especially of
males who try to impress by acting macho.

FLOW
To RAP very well.

FLY
A dance popular in the 1970s.

FLY¹

1) Exciting, dazzling, upscale, in the know. 2) Attractive.
See also ON THE FLY, SUPERFLY.

FLY²

See JET (newer term). See also TRUCKIN.

FOE-BY

A four-wheel-drive vehicle; a 4 × 4 jeep. *Foe* is "Four" rendered in AAE pronunciation; see Introduction.

FOE DAY

Before daybreak. "Before day" rendered in AAE pronunciation; see Introduction.

FOE-ONE-ONE (4-1-1)

The facts, the information on something, the DEAL. From the telephone number 4 1 1, used to get local directory assistance from the telephone company (a number now in the process of transition). A 1960s term resurfacing in HIP HOP, as in Mary J. Blige's 1992 album and title song *What's the 4 1 1?* First used in African American music by Aretha Franklin: "Now, Kitty, you know when we talk, we have a lot of fun, don't we, girl? Dishing out the dirt on everybody and giving each other the 4 1 1 on who drop kicked who this week" (from "Jump to It," the title JAM on her 1982 album, written and produced by Luther Van-

By permission of the artist, Craig Re

dross). "Four-one-one" rendered in AAE pronunciation; see Introduction.

FOLK / FOLKS

1) African Americans. 2) A generic term for gang members, used particularly by those in prison to conceal their identity as gang members from prison authorities.

FOLKS

The name of a gang in southeastern Michigan.

FOR DAYS

1) For a very long time, so long that you've lost track of the time. "I couldn't get nothin done cause she stayed here for days." 2) A lot of. "At this club, there was cowboys for days."

FOR THE DURATION

For the remaining life or existence of something. "I thought she was going to be out of the country for the duration," said in reference to a Black expatriate, meaning, for the rest of her life. Crossover expression.

FORE DAY

See FOE DAY.

FORGET IT / YOU / THAT / etc.

See FUHGIT IT / YOU / THAT / etc.

FORTY

A forty-ounce bottle of malt liquor, which has higher alcohol content than beer; mostly sold in urban, inner-city HOODS. Also *forty dog, forty ounce.*

FORTY ACRES

See FORTY ACRES AND A MULE.

FORTY ACRES AND A MULE

Symbolic of reparations for enslavement; a recurring phrase in Black Culture and throughout the African American Experience since the Civil War. Filmmaker Spike Lee uses this phrase as the name of his production company. In 1865,

Black preachers and other leaders of Savannah, Georgia, met with Union General William T. Sherman and indicated that freedom meant having their own land. Sherman issued an order for each ex-enslaved family to receive forty acres of land in coastal South Carolina and Georgia, and for the army to loan them mules. In 1866, Congress attempted to make Sherman's Special Field Order No. 15 official goverment policy by the passage of a bill strengthening the Freedmen's Bureau and authorizing it to make forty acres of land from confiscated Confederate property available to each household of ex-slaves. This legislation was designed to make them self-sufficient and to compensate for 246 years of free labor. At the time of President Lincoln's Emancipation Proclamation, the four million "freedmen" had nothing, not even any homes. However, this opportunity to establish a base of self-sufficiency for themselves and for future generations was not to be realized. President Andrew Johnson vetoed the bill, and Congress was unwilling, or unable, to override the veto. The total value of the *forty acres* today is estimated to be between three hundred and five hundred billion dollars. The Reparations Movement was recently reactivated with the establishment of N'COBRA (National Coalition of Blacks for Reparations), headquartered in D.C., and the introduction of Congressional bill H.R. 40 by Congressman John Conyers. The bill calls for the establishment of a commission to study the reparations issue, enslavement from 1619 to 1865, and the impact of over one hundred years of racial segregation since 1877 (the end of Reconstruction). Although "and a mule" does not appear in the 1866 bill, the phrase results from Sherman's actions, combined with the wording in Congress's bill about "provisions and supplies" to be issued to the "suffering freedmen." Also FORTY ACRES, FIFTY DOLLARS, AND A MULE.

FORTY ACRES, FIFTY DOLLARS, AND A MULE
See FORTY ACRES AND A MULE.

FORTY DOG
See FORTY.

FORTY OUNCE
See FORTY.

FOUL
1) Wrong; describes something that is not done properly. 2) Unprincipled. 3) Self-destructive.

FOUR-BY
See FOE-BY.

FOUR-ONE-ONE
See FOE-ONE-ONE.

FOX
A good-looking female. Also *stallion, star.*

FOXY
Good-looking, attractive; used for females. Crossover term.

FREAK
1) A person, male or female, whose sexual practices have no limitations, who will do anything sexually. 2) A generic term for any female; resented by most women when used by men.

FREEBASE
See BASE.

FREESTYLE
1) To perform spontaneous, unrehearsed RAP. 2) To DO ONE'S OWN THANG, wear one's own unique style of clothes or haircut, etc.

FRESH
See DEF.

FRIED, DYED, AND LAID TO THE SIDE
Describes hair that has been artificially STRAIGHTENed (*fried*) using a HOT COMB, creating a style with the hair

pressed close to the head; the hair may also be dyed a loud, flashy color, such as flaming red, blond, etc.

FRO

See AFRO.

FROG

A promiscuous person; one who hops and jumps—like a frog—into anybody's bed.

FROGGY

See IF YOU FEEL FROGGY, LEAP!

FROM GIDDYUP / GIDDAYUP

See FROM JUMPSTREET.

FROM JUMPSTREET

From the beginning point of something; from the start. Also *from Giddyup/Giddayup, from the Git-Go, from the Jump/from Jump, from the Rip.*

FROM THE GIT-GO

Crossover expression. See FROM JUMPSTREET.

FROM THE JUMP / FROM JUMP

See FROM JUMPSTREET.

FROM THE RIP

See FROM JUMPSTREET.

FRONT[1]

1) A fraudulent person; someone who's not for real. 2) Gold caps on the front teeth. Also *gold front, mouthpiece.*

FRONT[2]

1) To pretend. 2) To confront someone about something they supposedly are doing or should have done (older usage). Also *front somebody off, put somebody on front street.*

FRONT AND CENTER

Right this minute.

FRONT ON SOMEBODY

To deceive someone.

FRONT SOMEBODY OFF
See FRONT[2].

FRONT STREET
The state of being on public display, vulnerable to attack or accusation, including physical attack; a position of accountability for one's words and/or deeds. See also PUT SOMEBODY ON FRONT STREET.

FRUIT
The Fruit of Islam, the security force of the Nation of Islam (see The NATION).

FRY
To STRAIGHTEN the hair using a HOT COMB.

FUCK[1]
Used in reference to various non-sexual events to show emphasis or indicate disapproval. "I don't give a fuck," meaning, I do not care, it is irrelevant to me; "What in the fuck did you think you was doin?" meaning, What you did was extraordinarily wrong.

FUCK[2]
Used to dismiss something or someone as irrelevant or unimportant, in the sense of "forget that." See also FUHGIT IT / YOU / THAT / etc.

FUCKED UP
1) Drunk on liquor or high on drugs. 2) Confused, disorganized, distraught because of something that has occurred. 3) Beaten up.

FUHGIT IT / YOU / THAT / HIM / etc.
Euphemism for *fuck it/you/that/him/etc.* This expression uses the word "forget," rendered according to the pronunciation system of AAE; see Introduction.

FULL FACE
A complete application of makeup to the face, including the eyes and mouth.

FULL OF SHIT

Describes a person who is empty, full of nothing, who talks a good game but doesn't produce or follow through.

FUNDS

Money.

FUNK

1) The musical sound of jazz, blues, work songs, rhythm and blues, and African American music generally. 2) The quality of being SOULful, FUNKY. 3) A bad smell; an unpleasant odor. 4) Euphemism for *fuck,* in its sexual meaning.

FUNKY

1) Very SOULful. 2) In touch with the fundamental essence of life; in touch with one's body and spirit. 3) Describes the musical sound of FUNK. 4) Having a bad smell, an unpleasant odor. 5) Acting unpleasant, disagreeable.

FUNKY FRESH

Describes something that is super, exceptional, superior to FRESH.

G

G

1) A form of address for a male, usually one who is HIP or DOWN. Probably the AAE version of "guy." Also *man* (older term); *money* (newer term). 2) A woman a man has a relationship with.

G

To have sex.

G-RIDE

A stolen car.

G THANG

1) A reference to an experience, feeling, way of thinking, event, etc., that pertains to males, usually those who are DOWN. 2) A GANGSTA Thang.

GAFFLE

1) To rob, steal. 2) To cheat; run a con or scam on somebody. Also *gank*.

GAME

1) A series of activities and maneuvers to achieve a goal. 2) A story or RAP for obtaining what you want, used for manipulative and deceptive purposes. 3) A style of carrying and expressing oneself that enables one to achieve a desired end; to lack this style is referred to as "not having any *game*." 4) Criminal activities.

GANGBANGER

See BANGER.

GANGBANGIN

Belonging to a gang and participating in its activities. Also *bangin*.

GANGSTA

1) Used to refer to any event, activity, behavior, person, or object that represents a rejection of mainstream society's standards. 2) A rebellious, nonconformist person, a social "outlaw" who refuses to buckle under to white authority and white norms and is thus revered. Both these meanings reflect a resurfacing and extension of the 1960s and 1970s concept of *gangsta*, referring to street life and street culture. 3) Marijuana. Also *ganja* (newer term, showing Caribbean influence).

GANGSTA CLASS

Characteristic of GANGSTAS; COOL; DOWN.

GANGSTA LEAN

A posture of leaning to the right side and slouching down while driving a car.

GANGSTA LIMP

A male style of walking or strutting with a slight dip in the stride; projecting a COOL, FLY, HIP image by the style of walking. Also *gangsta walk;* and *pimp walk, pimp strut, cat walk, catting* (older terms).

GANGSTA ROLL

A large wad of paper money; a lot of money carried on the person.

GANGSTA WALK

See GANGSTA LIMP.

GANGSTA WALLS

White sidewall car tires; considered flamboyant and FLY; very popular in the 1960s and 1970s.

GANJA

Marijuana. Also *ganja weed; gangsta* (older term).

GANJA WEED

See GANJA.

GANK

See GAFFLE.

GANKER

See DECOY.

GAP MOUTH[1]

Describes a person who has a space (*gap*) between the upper middle two front teeth; perceived as sensual and sexy. Also *gap tooth.*

GAP MOUTH[2]

1) A person who tells your business; a "big mouth." 2) A person who has a reputation for performing oral sex.

GAP TOOTH

See GAP MOUTH[1].

GAT

A gun. Older term resurfacing in HIP HOP. Also *gauge.*

GATORS

Shoes made from alligator skins; very expensive, and popular as a symbol of success, especially among males.

GAUGE

See GAT.

G'D UP

Dressed up, according to whatever one's standards are. Probably a resurfacing and modification of GEARED UP (older term).

GEAR

Clothes. Probably a resurfacing and variation of GEARED UP (older term).

GEARED UP

See G'D UP (newer term).

GEE MO NITTY!

An expression of exasperation or bewilderment. "How many times I gotta explain it? Gee mo nitty!"

GEEK[1]

An unHIP person; a SQUARE.

GEEK[2] / GEEK UP

In a general state of exuberance, enthusiasm, excitement about something. Also *amp* (newer term). AAE pronunciation of "geeked"; see Introduction.

GELEE (PRONOUNCED GAY-LAY)

A turban-style African headwrap worn by women.

...mission of the artist, Craig Rex Perry, and *Young Sisters and Brothers Magazine.*

GET A NUT, GET BUSY, etc.
    See GIT A NUT, GIT BUSY, etc.

GHOST
    See DO A GHOST, GIT GHOST.

GIDDYUP / GIDDAYUP
    See JUMPSTREET.

GIFT
    See SHOOT THE GIFT.

GIG
    1) A dance or party. 2) In the lingo of jazz musicians, a job; a booking. 3) Any job. This meaning has crossed over.

GIG ON
    1) To play with; to make a fool of. 2) To deceive a person.

GIRL
    1) A way of addressing a female; used mostly between women, although it can be used by men with women friends. "Boy," by contrast, cannot be used as a form of address for males over eight or nine years old. 2) A generic reference to any female. 3) One's close friend. 4) Any female, not necessarily personally known, with whom one shares solidarity or whom one admires; a role model; used with *my, your, her,* etc. 5) Cocaine.

GIRLFRIEND
    A form of address for, or reference to, any female.

GIT A NUT
    To have an orgasm; used in reference to either a male or female. See also BUS ONE'S NUTS.

GIT BUSY
    To start to do something—to party, talk, work, etc.; to begin to take care of business.

GIT CLIPPED
    To be deceived or cheated, usually out of money. Crossover expression.

GIT DOWN

To do something enthusiastically and vigorously, such as dance, sing, work, or talk.

GIT GHOST

To keep a low profile.

GIT-GO

See JUMPSTREET. "When you settin up your own business, it's the Git-Go that kills you."

GIT GOOD TO SOMEBODY

To get carried away while doing something that starts out in a routine fashion. "He [the hairdresser] was jes suppose to be cuttin off a lil bit of hair so we could get this hairstyle, and it got good to him; next thang I know, I'm bald-headed!"

GIT HAPPY

To be overcome with religious ecstasy; to be possessed by the Holy Spirit. Expressed by shouting, crying with joy, religious/holy dancing, TALKIN IN TONGUE. Also *git the Spirit.*

GIT IT ON

To start something enthusiastically, especially sex, a party, or a fight.

GIT IT TOGETHA

To compose oneself; to pull things together to achieve a purpose; to do things the way they should be done. Crossover expression. See also TOGETHA, which has not crossed over.

GIT MINE / YOURS / HIS / HERS/ etc.

To obtain one's share of something; to get or take what is due you. Also *go for self / yours / his / hers / etc.*

GIT OFF MY CASE

Stop nagging me; stop pestering me about some situation. Crossover expression. See also CASE, ON SOMEBODY'S CASE.

GIT ON THE GOOD FOOT

To correct whatever needs improving; to put your best foot forward; to straighten out things. Popularized by James Brown's 1972 JAM.

GIT OUT MY FACE

Stop confronting me; remove yourself from my presence; I don't want to hear it. Crossover expression. See also GIT UP IN SOMEBODY'S FACE.

GIT OUTA HERE!

A response of enthusiasm or surprise.

GIT OVAH

1) A Traditional Black Church term referring to making it over to the spiritual side of life, having struggled and overcome sin. "My soul look back and wonder how I got ovah." 2) By extension, to overcome racism, oppression, or any obstacle in the way of your goal.

GIT OVAH ON

To deceive somebody; to fool.

GIT PAID

1) To obtain money, regardless of the means. 2) To have a steady income.

GIT REAL

To get serious; to stop fantasizing and dealing in illusions. Crossover expression.

GIT SKINS

To have sex. Also *hit the skins*. See also IN THE SKINS.

GIT SOME AIR

To go outside; to leave a place.

GIT SOME BOODY

1) To have sex with a woman. 2) To have anal sex, especially male-to-male.

GIT SOME LEG

To have sex with a woman.

GIT THE ASS
> To get angry.

GIT THE SPIRIT
> To be overcome with religious ecstasy; to be possessed by the Holy Spirit. Also *git happy.*

GIT UP
> To leap and jump high, especially in B-BALL. See also HOPS.

GIT UP IN SOMEBODY'S FACE
> To confront or argue with somebody face-to-face; to show disapproval of someone's actions while positioning oneself in close proximity to that person. See also GIT OUT MY FACE.

GIT WASTED
> To get drunk on liquor; sometimes, to get extremely high on marijuana. See also FUCKED UP.

GIT WIT
> 1) To establish a relationship with someone. 2) To desire or try to have sex with someone. 3) To participate in or go along with something. "You can git wit this or you can git wit that."

GIVE A CARE
> Euphemism for *give a shit.*

GIVE IT UP
> 1) To surrender a position or territory in competitive play. 2) To have sex. This meaning is also expressed as *give up the ass.*

GIVE SOME HEAD
> To perform oral sex on a man.

GIVE SOMEBODY FIVE
> To slap someone's hand in greeting, to show strong agreement, etc. Also *give somebody skin/some skin.* See also FIVE.

GIVE SOMEBODY SKIN / SOME SKIN
   See GIVE SOMEBODY FIVE.

GIVE SOMEBODY SOME PLAY
   To flirt; to show romantic interest in somebody.

GIVE SOMEBODY SOME SLACK
   See CUT SOMEBODY SOME SLACK.

GIVE SOMEBODY SOME SUGAR
   To kiss.

GIVE SOMETHING SOME PLAY
   To show interest in and give one's attention to something.

GIVE UP THE ASS
   See GIVE IT UP.

GLASS DICK
   The pipe used to smoke crack.

GLASS HOUSE
   A house where crack is sold; a drug house.

GO BACK
   Used in reference to the return of STRAIGHTENed hair to its natural, curly (KINKY, NAPPY) state, due to exposure to water, sweat, or other types of dampness or moisture.

GO DOWN
   To happen, occur, take place. "What went down was . . . "; "Now this is what's gon go down."

GO DOWN ON
   To perform oral sex on someone.

GO FOR
   1) To believe or accept something. "I'll go for that." 2) To be taken in or deceived by an action or verbal persuasion. "Since they went for my story, everythang turned out okay."

GO FOR BAD
   1) Refers to a person who projects an image of toughness and fighting ability. 2) By extension, refers to a person who projects an image of badness or toughness in any area.

GO FOR SELF / YOURS / HIS / HERS / etc.
> See GIT MINE / YOURS / HIS / HERS / etc.

GO FOR WHAT YOU KNOW
> To execute a move, play, or action that you have expertise in, particularly in a conflict or a threatening or tense situation.

GO OFF
> 1) To lose control. 2) To perform anything outstandingly, taking it to another level.

GO OUT
> To die or be killed.

GO OUT LIKE A SUCKER
> To die as the result of a drug overdose or gang violence.

GO OVAH
> To endure the secret ritual that initiates one into a fraternity or sorority. The ritual itself is called CROSS THE BURNING SANDS. Also *cross ovah*.

GO TO BLOWS
> To fight vigorously or viciously.

GO UPSIDE SOMEBODY'S HEAD
> To hit or slap someone on the head.

GOD DON'T LIKE UGLY
> A popular saying from the Oral Tradition, meaning that some negative action, behavior, or attitude is displeasing to the Creator, and you will be punished.

GOLD DIGGER
> A woman who runs after men for their money; emerging also as a term for a man who pursues women for money. An older general slang term resurfacing in HIP HOP Culture. Also *sack chaser* (newer term).

GOLD FRONT
> See FRONT[1].

GONE
> Euphemism for *dead*. "My daddy been gone a year now."

GONE HOME
   See HOME.

GOOD
   Said with emphasis, refers to someone or something that is
   excellent or superb, not simply "good."

GOOD HAIR
   Hair that is not naturally tightly curled, but naturally
   straight or slightly wavy; hair akin to that of whites. According to Black woman writer and anthropologist Zora
   Neale Hurston (author of the 1937 novel *Their Eyes Were
   Watching God*), *good hair* was also once referred to as
   nearer, my God, to thee. AFRICAN-CENTERED and activist FOLK reject this concept. See also BAD HAIR.

GOOD TO GO
   Ready to participate in an activity or event; predisposed to
   do or agree with something.

GOT HIS / HER NOSE
   A person who has another person vulnerable, helplessly
   and hopelessly in love with him or her is said to have *got*
   that person's *nose*. See also GOT HIS / HER NOSE OPEN.

GOT HIS / HER NOSE OPEN
   Refers to a person who is vulnerable and helpless because
   of being deeply in love. *Nose open* derives from the idea of
   the scent or smell of sex; it is this that "opens the nose."
   Got his nose open was used by former D.C. Mayor Marion
   Barry in a conversation with his ex-girlfriend, Rasheeda
   Moore. Noting the expensive watch she was wearing,
   which she had gotten as a present from her new boyfriend,
   Barry said to her, "You got his nose open, huh?" The FBI,
   which recorded the conversation, misinterpreted the statement as referring to cocaine use.

GOT IT GOIN ON
   Superbly or effectively doing something; refers to a success-
   ful or competent person or thing. "That new beautician,

she got it goin on"; "Mickey D up there got it goin on this week."

GOT YOUR BACK

An expression of support for a friend or comrade in any situation, event, plan, or scheme. From the idea of protecting the person against surprise "attack" by adversaries coming unexpectedly from the "rear."

GRANDSTAND

1) To talk BAD in a loud, aggressive, flashy manner. 2) To dress and act in a flamboyant manner so as to attract attention. 3) To show off. Also *showboat*.

GRAPEVINE

A source of information or news through the informal verbal networks of the community. Crossover term.

GRAY

A fairly neutral term for a white person; however, possibly from the gray color of Confederate army uniforms, and if so, originally must have referred to white racial supremacists.

GREASE

To eat.

GREAT WHITE HOPE

A white person on whom European Americans are depending to excel in a field where African Americans dominate.

GRITS

1) Food of any kind. 2) Money. 3) One's business.

GROWN

Used to describe a young male or female who is acting and/or looking like an adult; generally used in a negative sense. "She is too grown for me" (said in reference to a ten-year-old girl conducting herself like an adult woman).

GSP

Golden shower people, that is, people who pee on you; wrongdoers, obviously not serving your best interests.

GUMBY¹

Awkward, silly-looking.

GUMBY²

A hairstyle in which the hair is worn to one side. Derived from the cartoon character "Gumby," who has been wearing his hair that way for decades.

GUT BUCKET

A "low-class" bar, club, or other place of entertainment. Blues music is sometimes described as *gut bucket* music.

H

HA-STEP

To do something halfway, not putting your maximum into it. From the AAE pronunciation of "half-step"; see Introduction.

HAIM

A job. Also *slave*.

HAINCTY

Unpleasant, contentious; picky and petty; commonly used in reference to females who act this way.

HAIR DRESSED

Used in reference to getting one's hair done or styled.

HALF-STEP

See HA-STEP.

HALF TRACK

A quantity of crack purchased by the SMOKER, approximately $125 worth.

HAMMER

1) A good-looking woman; emerging as a term for a good-looking man also. 2) See BARS.

HAND

In BID, a round of play. See also SETTIN HAND.

HANDKERCHIEF HEAD

An UNCLE TOM–type person who defers to European Americans and their authority; may also act against the interests of Black people. Also *Tom, Uncle Tom, Uncle Thomas; Aunt Thomasina, Aunt Jane.*

HANDS DOWN

Of course, naturally. Older term resurfacing.

HANG

1) To party. Also *hang out.* 2) To endure or tolerate something. "I can't hang with that." 3) To stay put, remain somewhere. "Why don't you hang a while?"

HANG OUT

See HANG.

HAPPY

See GIT HAPPY.

HARD

Describes a person who is tough, hardened by life and experience.

HARD-HEADED

Describes a person who refuses to listen to reason or obey a command, as in the proverb "A hard head make a soft behind."

HARD LEG

A male.

HARD ROCK

A generic term for any hardened, strong, tough person.

HAT UP

To leave. Probably derived from the act of putting on one's hat when leaving to go outside.

HAWK

Extremely cold weather, made more so by the wind-chill factor. Also *Mista Wind, Joe Chilly.*

HAWKING

Staring at someone.

HE-SAY-SHE-SAY

1) Gossip. 2) Any statement that can't be verified; word-of-mouth, loose talk; hearsay in general.

HEAD

The end of the penis. See also GIVE SOME HEAD.

HEAD HUNTER

A woman who performs sex with men for drugs, or for money to buy drugs. Probably derived from the use of HEAD in referring to the penis. Also *strawberry*.

HEAD RAG

1) A scarf or handkerchief worn around the head to indicate gang affiliation. 2) A scarf, handkerchief, or STOCKING CAP tied around the hair to keep it in place and preserve one's hairstyle. *Head rag* refers to such a head covering worn by a male or female; DO-RAG, however, refers only to a head covering worn by males.

HEAD-UP

Refers to a competition or confrontation of any kind—e.g., cards, basketball, a fight—involving just two opponents, ONE-ON-ONE. "Me and old Mose just sat there all night playin stud poker, head-up."

HEADS

1) One's children. 2) A generic reference to African Americans; possibly derived from a reference to hair, generally of major importance to Blacks.

HEAT

A gun. An older general slang term resurfacing in the usage of gang members.

HEAVY

1) Describes a person who is a profound thinker, or one with highly developed leadership skills. 2) Describes a per-

son who has a high-status position at a job or in an organization. This meaning has crossed over.

HEIFER

A reference to any female; used by males or females; a fairly neutral term.

HELLIFIED

Describes an unusual style or manner of doing something, unconventional but highly admirable. "You sho got a hellified way of explaining things."

HELLO!

A response of affirmation.

HELLO?

A call for an affirmative response, that is, Do you agree with me? Do you hear what I'm saying?

HERB

Marijuana. Crossover term.

HIGH

A state of excitement or exuberance, usually, but not necessarily, induced by liquor or drugs. Crossover term. See also NATURAL HIGH, which has not crossed over.

HIGH FIVE

A FIVE with the hands held high. Crossover expression and ritual.

HIGH ROLLER

1) A big-time drug dealer. 2) Anyone engaged in any big illegal moneymaking scheme.

HIGH TOP FADE

See FADE[1].

HIGH YELLUH

See YELLUH.

HIP[1]

1) Knowledgeable, aware of something; with-it. From Wolof *hipi*, literally, "to open one's eyes." Crossover meaning. 2) See HYPE[1], DEF.

HIP²

To inform someone or make someone aware of something. "They hipped me to what was goin down."

HIP HOP

Urban youth culture, associated with RAP Music, break dancing, graffiti; probably derived from the partying style of DJS playing hype ("hip") music at a dance ("hop"). Three different New York entertainers have been credited with coining the term in the 1970s: Busy Bee Starski, DJ Hollywood, and DJ Afrika Bambaataa. However, according to Kool DJ Herc, the acknowledged father of Hip Hop, "only these three could argue it."

HIT¹

1) A romantic overture, designed to make the person your MAN or WOMAN. See also HIT ON. 2) A win in the lottery or NUMBER GAME. See also HIT THE NUMBER/LOTTERY. 3) An ingestion of drugs, usually heroin; older meaning that has crossed over.

HIT²

In a card game, to request that the dealer give you a card from the deck. "Hit me."

HIT IT

1) To smoke, usually in reference to marijuana or crack. 2) To have sex.

HIT ON

To make romantic overtures toward someone.

HIT THE NUMBER / LOTTERY

To win in the NUMBER GAME or lottery.

HIT THE SKINS

See GIT SKINS.

HNIC

Head Nigger in Charge; a Black person put in charge by whites, usually not in charge of anything meaningful; generally functions to keep other Blacks in line. Also *BNIC* (Boss Nigger in Charge).

HO

1) A generic reference to any female, used by males and females; women use the term to refer to close friends and intimates, as well as to antagonists and rivals. Despite its common usage in RAP and HIP HOP and the fact that it has neutral as well as negative meanings, *ho* remains a controversial word. Derived from the AAE pronunciation of "whore"; see Introduction. The film *House Party* projects the humor in lack of understanding of the rules of AAE in a scene where a white teacher is reprimanding a Black male student with the question, "Why did you call his mother a garden tool?" The teacher had heard *ho* as "hoe," not "whore." 2) A reference to a male or female who engages in sex indiscriminately. 3) A reference to a female who engages in sex for free (older meaning). In this sense, the *ho* is contrasted with the prostitute, who is perceived as more principled because she works for a living, i.e., she engages in sex as a business.

Ho! Ho!

An expression used at a party, dance, or other lively social event, suggesting a call to all present to PAR-TAY.

HOE

See HO.

HOG

A Cadillac car.

HOG MAWS

The stomach of a pig, eaten as a delicacy; not as expensive as CHITLINS, but pretty costly, nonetheless.

HOLDING DOWN

Controlling turf or an area, according to gang talk.

HOLE

In basketball, the basket.

HOLLA

To shout, holler.

HOLLER

See HOLLA.

HOME

1) A generic reference to any area south of the Mason-Dixon Line, the original U.S. "home" to the African enslaved population and the birthplace of virtually the entire Black population from Emancipation until the Great Migration out of the South after World Wars I and II. Thus, "My momma nem went home last month" does not refer to the current home of the speaker, but to a place in the South where the speaker and her family are from. Also *down home.* 2) A generic reference to a person of African descent. 3) By extension, any place or thing associated with NITTY-GRITTY Blackness. 4) A Traditional Black Church reference to a spiritual Home in Heaven. "I got a Home not built by worldly hands." Funeral services are referred to as *Homegoing* celebrations. The SAVED person who dies is said to have *gone Home.* Also *Home on High.* 5) See HOMEY.

HOME ON HIGH

See HOME.

HOME SLICE

1) A Black person; Black people. 2) See HOMEY.

HOMEFOLKS

1) Black people; a Black person. 2) See HOMEY.

HOMEGIRL / HOMEBOY

1) A fellow gang member. 2) A Black person. 3) See HOMEY.

HOMEGOING

See HOME.

HOMES

1) A Black person; Black people. 2) See HOMEY.

HOMEY

1) A person from one's neighborhood. Also *homegirl/ homeboy*. Crossover terms and meaning. Also *homes, home, home slice*, and *homefolks*, terms which have not crossed over. 2) A Black person. Also *homegirl/homeboy, homes, home, home slice, homefolks*. This use of these words has not crossed over.

HOMO

A derogatory term for a gay male.

HONKY

A negative term for a white person. Probably derived and borrowed from the name-calling and expression of resentment by settled European Americans against central and Eastern European immigrants, who were negatively referred to as "hunkies" (from *Hungarians*). Blacks, in competition with these immigrants in the first half of the twentieth century, generalized the term to all whites. Also *hunky*.

HOOCHIE

A sexually promiscuous female.

HOOD

1) Neighborhood, especially the neighborhood where you live or have grown up; your roots and a place where you feel welcome and at home. 2) Short for *hoodlum*, a rowdy, aggressive, hard-nosed, street-fighting type of man or woman.

HOODOO

The negative component of the VOODOO religion.

HOODOO MAN

A male supposedly skilled in the art and practice of the magical system of the VOODOO religion, which was transplanted to the United States (also the Caribbean and Latin America) from West Africa during enslavement. A distortion of the role of the Voodoo priest and a mockery of the extensive knowledge, training, and experience of the

Voodoo healer/doctor. The *hoodoo man* claims to be able to cure any sickness, put on and/or remove hexes from people, increase one's sexual prowess, predict the number (see NUMBERS), etc.—all for a fee, of course. The number of *hoodoo men* is not as great as it once was, but they are still to be found in the COMMUNITY. Although there were and are *hoodoo* women, the practice of HOODOO has been largely dominated by males.

HOOK

1) A phony; an imitation. 2) The police.

HOOK SOMETHING UP

To create, design, or arrange something; to fix something up according to one's own style or TIP, as in decorating, or *hooking up,* an apartment or house, selecting and coordinating a wardrobe or an outfit, restyling an old car, setting up a special pleasure trip, etc.

HOOK-UP

Anything attractive, artistic, or great that a person has put together that reflects his/her own style, such as a stylish outfit, a beautifully decorated CRIB, a unique business card, a creative answering machine message, etc.

HOOKED

Describes something or someone that is attractive, tastefully put together, upscale.

HOOP¹

See B-BALL¹. See also TAKE IT TO THE HOOP.

HOOP²

1) See B-BALL². Also *shoot some hoop.* 2) To laugh loud and heartily. "They was jes hoopin and hollin when I got there."

HOOPTY

An old, broken-down car.

HOO-RAH

A lot of noise; loud talk. "Yall cut out all that hoo-rah."

HOPS

The ability to leap and jump high, especially in B-BALL. "That Brotha got good hops." Also *springs* (newer term); *rise, sky* (older terms). See also GIT UP.

HOT

1) Refers to music, usually jazz, that is very fast-tempoed and played with fervor and high energy, the speed generating "heat." Probably from Mandingo *goni*, literally, "hot," also "fast." 2) By extension, refers to high energy generated in any activity. "The Lakers done got hot now," suggesting that they're starting to play great basketball. 3) Sexually aroused. 4) Stolen goods.

HOT-BLOODED

Describes a person, often female, with high sexual energy, a person whose libido is stronger than average. Also *hot-natured*. See also A LOT OF NATURE.

HOT COMB

A heated metal comb used to STRAIGHTEN hair. Also *hot iron*.

HOT IRON

See HOT COMB.

HOT-NATURED

See HOT-BLOODED.

HOT SAUCE

A peppery sauce, very hot and spicy. Believed to be from a recipe dating to enslavement that was possibly brought over from Africa. Marketed commercially today; distinct in taste from the popular European American version of *hot sauce* (Tabasco sauce).

HOUND

A promiscuous man; derived from many women's perception of men as "dogs who will fuck anythang," a view depicted in the "Women's War Council" scene in Spike Lee's 1991 film *Jungle Fever*.

HOUSE

   1) To take something from somebody; to take over, exert one's power. 2) See CLOWN[1].

HOUSE NIGGA

   See FIELD NIGGA.

HUMP

   To have sex. Crossover term. A male in the act of lovemaking is said to have A HUMP IN HIS BACK, an expression that has not crossed over.

HUMP IN HIS BACK

   See HUMP.

HUMPIN

   1) Very attractive; good-looking. 2) See DEF.

HUNG

   Used to describe a male whose penis is large. Crossover term. Also *hung low,* which has not crossed over.

HUNG LOW

   See HUNG.

HUNKY

   See HONKY.

HUSH YO MOUF!

   A response of surprise; a reaction to startling or incredible information.

THE HUSTLE

   1) A popular group dance, done in a line formation. Also *the Electric Slide, the Bus Stop, the Madison* (older terms, same dance). 2) An older dance done by couples (New York).

HUSTLE

   A scheme or work, either legal or illegal, for obtaining money.

HUSTLER

   One who survives and makes money by deviousness and schemes, usually illegal but nonviolent, such as by various gambling games involving the NUMBERS, shooting pool, PICK-UP basketball GAMES, etc.

HYPE[1]

See DEF. Probably a resurfacing of and variation on *hip* (older term).

HYPE[2]

Deceptive, propagandistic statements or stories, particularly European American propaganda.

I

ICE[1]

A new synthetic drug that is potentially explosive; not as strong as CAT.

ICE[2]

1) Describes a person who is bold, daring, calculating, in control, superCOOL. 2) Refers to a person who speaks the plain, unvarnished, cold, hard truth. "Did you hear what she said? Ice, baby, ice." Current Rappers' names and lyrics symbolize this quality—"Ice Cube," "Ice-T," even "Vanilla Ice."

ICE[3]

To kill.

ICE PEOPLE

White people, from a perception of whites as cold and ruthless. According to some Black Nationalist ideologies, Caucasians lived in cold climes in Europe and thus developed a cold, inhumane system of thought.

IF YOU FEEL FROGGY, LEAP!

Used as a challenge to fight.

IG

To ignore someone by refusing to speak or otherwise

acknowledge their presence. See also PUT THE IG ON.

ILL

See SICK.

ILLIN

See TRIPPIN.

IN EFFECT

Describes somebody or something that is present and operative in all his/her/its glory, a force to be reckoned with. "My crew is in effect."

IN LIKE FLIN

Accepted by a person or a group; well-received. From the James Bond–type character in the 1960s movie *Our Man Flint,* who GITS OVAH in the film. "Flint" becomes *Flin* through AAE pronunciation rules; see Introduction.

IN THE DAY

Refers to a past era that was the heyday of someone or something.

IN THE HOUSE

Indicates the presence of someone—that he or she is now here in our midst. "Yo! MC Too Smooth is in the house." And, "Yo, who's in the house?" the DJ asked. "MICKEY MOUSE IS IN THE HOUSE, AND DONALD DUCK DON'T GIVE A FUCK," the party people answered.

IN THE MIX

1) Refers to a DJ's synthesizing of or mixing together sounds from various records to create a new sound. 2) Interfering with a plan; involved in somebody's business. "Everythang was all right until she got in the mix." 3) Involved in gang activity.

IN THE SKINS

Having sex. See also GIT SKINS, HIT THE SKINS.

IN THE STREET

1) Not at home; on the go a lot. See also STAY IN THE STREET. 2) HANGing OUT, partying. See also RUN THE

STREET. 3) Describes a life style that is an alternative to the working-class style of the COMMUNITY.

IN THERE

Attractive, looking good.

IN YA FACE

1) In basketball, refers to a defensive player closely guarding, that is, "up in the face of," an offensive player. 2) Refers to making a basket on a defensive player in spite of all his attempts to prevent it, right under his nose, so to speak. 3) By extension, describes any issue, problem, or confrontation that has become personalized, or a crisis that has hit home. In the process of crossing over, as used in this sense.

J

JACK

A form of address for any male. "Hey, Jack, what's goin on?" (said to a man whose name is Harry). Also *G, B* (newer terms); *Bo-jack* (older term).

JACK^1

Short for JACK-SHIT, meaning "nothing." "They been workin all that time and ain got jack"; "I stayed with you all this time for what? You ain done jack-shit for me," meaning, You have given me nothing in this relationship, no emotional fulfillment, no psychological support, no material goods, nothing.

JACK^2

To take something from someone.

JACK MOVE

A wild action; a bizarre move or behavior.

JACK-SHIT

See JACK^1.

JACK UP

To beat up, assault somebody.

JACKLEG

1) An unprofessional or phony preacher. Because of the significance of the Church and preachers, who are believed to be "sent" or "called" by God, a *jackleg* is a grievous offense in and to the COMMUNITY. 2) Blacks extended the notion of the preacher as *jackleg* to include *any* person who pretends to be something that they're not, such as a *jackleg plumber,* a *jackleg mechanic,* a *jackleg carpenter,* etc. Also *shade tree.*

JAM¹

1) A song or recording. 2) A party.

JAM²

1) To confront someone. 2) To party; to dance. 3) What musicians do when they play with high energy and excitement. 4) To have sex. 5) To DUNK the ball in B-BALL.

JAM SESSION

A gathering of musicians playing HOTly, THROWing DOWN.

JAMMIN

See DEF.

JAMMY

A gun.

JAW JACKIN

Talking excessively; literally, "jackin off" at the mouth, or verbal masturbation. Recently used by Sam Perkins during the 1993 NBA playoff series; NBC commentators made special note of the term, thinking it was new, but it goes a long way back. Also *runnin off at the mouth.*

JAWS TIGHT

Describes somebody who is angry. "You messed up, Bro. Her jaws is tight now!"

JAZZ

Not only refers to the music, but is used as a verb meaning "to speed up, to excite, to act uninhibited." Possibly from Mandingo *jasi*, literally, "to act out of the ordinary." Originally, *jazz* referred to sexual activity.

JAZZY

Exciting, upscale, DOWN WITH the latest trends or fashions.

JEEP MUSIC

Good music, the kind that's good for PUMPin UP THE VOLUME and listening to while CHILLIN in your jeep.

JERK SOMEBODY AROUND

To run a scam or deception on somebody. Crossover expression.

JET

1) To run fast. Also *motor*, *fly* (older terms). See also TRUCKIN. 2) To leave.

JHERI-CURL

Also referred to as a *Jheri*, this is a style or look created by using a chemical relaxer that replaces the natural, tight curl of Black hair with a straighter curl that has a shiny, wet look. Thus treated, the hair is generally worn loose, either long or short, but with little variation in terms of style. From the name of the person, Jheri Redding, who invented the process and introduced it to African American hairdressers in the 1970s. The fact that the *Jheri* caught on so among Blacks was a surprise to many *beauticians*, and to the Redding family as well. Since that time, there have been many adaptations by other manufacturers, but the terms *Jheri* and *Jheri-Curl* continue to be used to refer to all such processes since all result in the *Jheri-Curl* look. Because of its heavy, oily texture, the *Jheri* (as well as its imitations) often leaves greasy spots on clothing and furniture, which became the source of humor and SIGNIFYIN in the 1988 film *Coming to America,* starring comic genius Eddie Murphy.

JIM / JIMMY

Penis. Also *Jim Browski, Jimmy joint.*

JIM BROWSKI

See JIM.

JIM / JIMMY HAT

A condom.

JIM JONES

1) To poison someone. 2) A cigarette containing cocaine and marijuana dipped in PCP. Derived from the name of the African American cult leader Jim Jones. In 1977 he fled the United States with about a thousand followers, ending up in Jonestown, Guyana, where they later committed mass suicide by drinking Kool-Aid spiked with potassium cyanide.

JIMMY JOINT

See JIM.

JINGLIN

Attractive, sexy; usually used in reference to women.

JITTERBUG

A superHIP, streetified person; the term is often used with a hint of scorn. From a fast popular dance done in the 1930s, suggesting a person who is fast and wild.

JIVE

1) Lacking in seriousness, not committed. 2) Deceptive, putting somebody on. Crossover term. See also SHUCKIN AND JIVIN.

JOCK

1) To ingratiate oneself with somebody by being overly involved in his world or by imitating her actions and behavior, often in an exaggerated way. 2) To approach somebody aggressively to establish a relationship.

JOCK STRAP

To be "on a man's *jock strap*" is to impose oneself on him, to intrude into his space. For the female version of this, see BRA STRAP.

JODY

Any man having an affair with another man's wife or WOMAN. Probably derived from the name given to men rejected or deferred by the draft during major wars in this century. Such men were believed to prey on the wives and girlfriends left behind by the men who went off to war.

JOE CHILLY

See HAWK.

JOHNSON

Penis.

JOINT

1) A marijuana cigarette. 2) One's home. See CRIB. 3) Prison. These three uses have crossed over. 4) A gun. This meaning has not crossed over.

JONES

1) A strong, overwhelming desire for anything you indulge in or acquire and never get enough of—money, sex, chocolate, gambling, clothes, etc. Originally referred to addiction to heroin or cocaine. 2) Penis.

JUICE[1]

1) Power. 2) A gun. 3) Liquor; older meaning that has crossed over.

JUICE[2]

1) To trick or swindle; con someone. 2) To kill.

JUMP

See JUMPSTREET.

JUMP BAD

To become aggressive, ready to fight and do battle, either verbally or physically.

JUMP SALTY

To get mad or angry. See also SALTY.

JUMPSTREET

The start; the beginning point of something. Also *Giddyup/ Giddayup, Git-Go, Jump, Rip*. See also FROM JUMP-STREET.

JUNETEENTH

The day, usually in mid to late June, when African Americans celebrate emancipation from enslavement; originally June 19, 1865, the date enslaved Africans in Texas learned that they had been freed. Although Lincoln's Emancipation Proclamation became effective January 1, 1863, the status of enslavement continued, on some plantations for more than two years, since many plantation owners did not inform their slaves of Lincoln's order. When Texas ex-slaves got the news, they instituted this annual celebration. *Juneteenth* is currently celebrated in some two hundred cities across the nation.

JUNGLE FEVER

Among African and European Americans, an obsession with a person of the opposite race based on racial myths and stereotypes and intensified by the lure of the unknown, due to continued racial separation. The concept was depicted in Spike Lee's 1991 movie *Jungle Fever*.

K

KEEP ON KEEPIN ON

A familiar expression in the Oral Tradition, a statement of encouragement to continue struggling and striving to reach a goal; despite adversity, setbacks, and failures, the triumph is in continuing to struggle, to *keep on keepin on* against the odds. Originated in the Traditional Black Church.

KENTE (PRONOUNCED KIN-TEE)

A fabric imported from West Africa, styled in a variety of ways and worn as ornamental dressing by African Americans; the garment of royalty in traditional Africa.

KIBBLES AND BITS

1) Cheap food. 2) Used in reference to a man who is not well-endowed, not HUNG.

KICK

1) To inform, to convey the facts about something. "Let me kick some knowledge about the situation"; "Let's kick the ballistics," that is, Let's look at the facts I'm going to present to you. 2) To do something intensely and with high energy.

KICK BACK

To relax; take it easy. In the process of crossing over. Also *chill, chill out.*

KICK BUTT

1) To outdo a person or a team in a competitive endeavor. "Shaq [of the Orlando Magic basketball team] and his boys kicked the Celtics' butt." 2) To excel in something. "Bloods

ssion of the artist, Craig Rex Perry, and *Young Sisters and Brothers Magazine.*

should be kickin butt in math cause it's our thang from Africa."

KICK DOWN

To establish a person in the drug business.

KICK IT

1) To RAP, to use strong talk. Also *kick it live.* 2) To have an affair outside of one's monogamous relationship. Also *kick it around* (older usage).

KICK IT AROUND

See KICK IT.

KICK IT LIVE

See KICK IT.

KICK THE BALLISTICS

See BALLISTICS, KICK.

KICK TO THE CURB

1) To reject someone who is trying to establish a relationship, who is HITtin ON you. 2) To end an established relationship with someone. "My boy got kicked to the curb."

KICKIN

1) Doing something intensely and with high energy. 2) See DEF.

KICKS

Shoes.

KID

Used by a speaker to refer to her/himself in the third person. "The Kid ain down for that," meaning, I don't approve of that.

KINKS

Extremely curly hair, the natural state of African American hair, curled so tightly it appears "woolly" (KINKY or NAPPY). Also *naps.*

KINKY

See KINKS. Also *nappy.*

KITCHEN

The hair at the nape of the neck, inclined to be the most curly (KINKY) and thus the hardest part of STRAIGHTENed hair to keep from GOing BACK.

KNOCK

To criticize something or someone; to DIS a person, idea, or thing.

KNOCK BOOTS

To have sex. Possibly from taking (*knockin*) off one's lover's boots before engaging in sex.

KNOCKED OFF

Arrested; busted for a crime. A resurfacing and extension of the older general slang expression *knock off*, meaning "to kill."

KNOT

A roll of money.

KNOW WHAT UHM SAYIN?

A call for a response from the listener.

L

LADY

A male's female lover/girlfriend/partner.

LAID

1) Stylishly dressed. Also *clean*. 2) High on liquor or drugs.

LALA LAND

Los Angeles.

LAME

A thing, event, or person that is out of step, unable to keep up, thus unHIP, not with-it.

LAMP

To hang out. Possibly from the idea of hanging out under street lamps on urban corners.

LARCENY

Negative feelings, hostility toward somebody.

LATER

An expression used to indicate Goodbye; I'm leaving. "Okay, Kwesi will be there. Later." Also *Catch you later* (older expression which has crossed over, but *Later* has not); and *Outtie 5000, outa here* (newer expressions).

LATER

Used to dismiss or disregard something or somebody. Referring to African American politicians and other officials who forget all about their people, the SISTA said, "See, once they get in office, they just act like 'later for y'all.'"

LAY DEAD

1) To wait. 2) To keep a low profile.

LAY IT DOWN FOR ME

Make it plain, explain it to me. Also *lay it on me.*

LAY IT ON ME

See LAY IT DOWN FOR ME.

LAY OUT

An easy activity. "This job is a lay out."

LAY PIPE

A reference to what the male does during sex.

LAY UP

To relax or lounge around, generally in bed with one's partner.

LAYIN IN THE CUT

Refers to something or someone that is hiding, surreptitiously waiting to catch or surprise you; lurking. "When they tell you yo cancer in remission, all that mean is that bad boy layin in the cut waitin for yo ass!"

LEAN

See GANGSTA LEAN.

LEAVE SOMEBODY HANGIN

To ignore a hand extended for a handshake or a FIVE.

LED BY THE HEAD OF ONE'S DICK

Used in reference to a man unduly influenced by sex, one whose judgment is clouded by his sexual desire.

LEG

See GIT SOME LEG.

LEGIT

Refers to anything that's authentic; real, not fake; describes something that's appropriate, in order, as it should be.

LET THE DOOR HIT YOU WHERE THE GOOD LORD SPLIT YOU!

Euphemism for "Get yo ass out of here!" (*split you* being a reference to "ass").

LET'S HAVE CHURCH!

A call to the congregation to liven up, begin to praise and sing, show emotion, "make a joyful noise."

LIFTS

Hydraulics on a car; installed usually on older cars, to elevate the car and make it possible for it to run on two or three wheels. "Drop the ass" refers to activating the *lifts* to lower the rear of the car and elevate the front. It costs from four to five thousand dollars to have *lifts* installed on a car.

LIGHT BREAD

White bread.

LIGHT INTO

To confront someone verbally; to tell a person off, set them straight. Crossover expression.

LIGHT-SKIN

See FAIR.

LIGHT UP

1) To light a marijuana cigarette or crack pipe. 2) To domi-

nate, especially in sports. "Michael Jordan lit up the Knicks for 54."

LIGHTEN UP

To reduce the verbal or psychological pressure.

LIGHTWEIGHT

Lacking in achievement; unimportant. "He wasn't nothin but a lightweight ball player noway." Crossover term.

LIKE THAT

Possessing whatever quality is suggested by a preceding statement. "You live in this fine crib?" "Yeah, cause I got it like that," that is, I am in possession of the finer things in life, such as a beautiful house; "Yo, Momma! Look at all that weight you lost since I last saw you!" "Yeah. It's like that, I got it like that," meaning, Yes, I have the discipline and fortitude to stick to a weight loss program and succeed.

LIKE TO

To have almost done something. "Momma like to drop the baby."

LIKE WHITE ON RICE

Clinging to or following something or somebody extremely closely or tenaciously. "Five-O was on my man like white on rice."

LINE DON'T LIE

In B-BALL games in the HOOD, used in reference to a decision determined by the outcome of shooting from an agreed-upon line. In the absence of referees, whenever a player calls a foul, the opposing player can challenge the call. The conflict is resolved by SHOOTing THE DIE, that is, by the act of shooting from the agreed-upon line (usually a line roughly equivalent to the distance from the basket to the top of the key in regulation b-ball). If the player makes the basket, then the call was legitimate, and both teams accept that truth has been established because the *line don't lie.*

LIP
> A defensive verbal response when under attack or when resisting a command. "Do what I told you, and don't give me no lip!" Crossover term.

LIPS
> The vagina.

LIQUID JUICE
> Liquor.

LISTEN UP!
> A call to listen carefully, to pay attention because the speaker is about to KICK some knowledge.

LIVE
> See ALL THE WAY LIVE (older form).

LIVER-LIPS
> Reddish purple–colored lips, also usually BIG LIPS. A negative term; but see BIG LIPS.

LIVIN HIGH OFF THE HOG
> Having an opulent life style; living big in a material sense. Literally, eating the upper parts of the hog, that is, the ribs, pork chops, etc., rather than the lower parts, that is, CHITLINS, pig feet, etc. Crossover expression. Also *big-timin it; livin large* (newer term).

LIVIN LARGE
> See LIVIN HIGH OFF THE HOG.

LIZARDS
> Shoes made from lizard skins; expensive, and popular as a symbol of success, especially among African American males.

LOCKS
> See DREADLOCKS.

LOCS (PRONOUNCED LOKES)
> Sunglasses. Also *shades* (older term that has crossed over).

LOK (PRONOUNCED LOKE)
> Messed up; loco; mentally unbalanced; fanatical.

LOOT

Money. Older term resurfacing.

LORD, HAVE MERCY!

A response of affirmation or surprise.

A LOT OF NATURE

Describes a person who has a high sex drive. See also HOT-BLOODED, HOT-NATURED.

LOUD TALK

To talk in such a way as to confront or embarrass someone publicly.

LOVE BONE

See BONE.

LOW

Describes a person who is maintaining a low profile; not flashy. See also TAKE LOW.

LOW FIVE

A FIVE with the hands held low. Probably originated when the HIGH FIVE crossed over and too many white folks started high-fivin.

LOW-LIFE

Refers to the seamy underside of people, events, or places; "low-class"; unscrupulous, without morals or principles.

LOW RATE

To downgrade something or someone. Also *rank*.

LP

A long-playing, large-size phonograph record (33 ⅓), rapidly being replaced by the cassette tape and the compact disc. Originally a trademark term, popularized by African Americans; a crossover term. See also EL PEE.

LUG

A DIS; an expression of CAPPIN or SIGNIFYIN; may be said seriously or in fun. See also DROP A LUG.

LYIN

The art of telling stories and anecdotes, RAPpin, telling

jokes; general clever conversation using the African American Verbal Tradition. Some stories are fictional, that is, literally "lies"; others may have a kernel of truth; all are raised to the level of broad and imaginative exaggeration by a storyteller, who must have a good memory and be verbally adept, clever, witty, and funny to hold the listeners' attention during conversations that may go on FOR DAYS.

M

MACARONI
   1) See MACK DADDY (newer term). 2) The name of a Midwestern gang, no longer in existence.
MACK[1]
   1) A man who can sweet-talk women. 2) A man who has lots of women; a PLAYER. 3) A man who manipulates women for money; a PIMP.
MACK[2]
   To hustle or exploit someone.
MACK DADDY
   A man who has a lot of women and PLAYS them; a PLAYER. Also *Macaroni* (older term).
MACKIN
   Refers to a man trying to HIT ON, GIT WIT, deepen his acquaintance with a woman to make her his.
MAD
   A lot of; very much. Also *crazy*.
THE MADISON
   See the HUSTLE.
MAIN MAN
   1) One's best friend. 2) Back-up; a person who GOT YOUR BACK.

MAKE BANK
To obtain money.

MAKE LIKE
See MAY LIKE.

MAKE SOMEBODY'S LOVE COME DOWN
To stimulate somebody sexually.

MAMMA JAMMA
Euphemism for MUTHAFUCKA.

THE MAN
1) The police. Crossover term. Also *five-O* (newer term that has not yet crossed over). 2) A male of distinction. "Michael Jordan is The Man." 3) The white man.

MAN
1) A woman's boyfriend/husband/partner; used by males and females. 2) A form of address for any male. Crossover term. Also *G, Money* (newer terms); *Jack, Bo-jack, Bo-dick* (older terms).

MANDINGO
A strong, usually big-built African American male; an allusion to the stereotype about the sexual powers of the Black man.

MANNISH
Used to reprimand a young male who is acting too grown-up and too much like an adult. Females acting too grown-up are said to be WOMLISH or WOMNISH.

MARK
A weak person, a pushover. Resurfacing and extension of older general slang term. "Musta thought I was sleazy or thought I was a mark cause I used to hang with Eazy" (from Dr. Dre's "Wit Dre Day," on his 1992 album *The Chronic*).

MARY FRANCES
Euphemism for MUTHAFUCKA.

MARY JANE
　Marijuana.

MARYLAND FARMER
　Euphemism for MUTHAFUCKA.

MAX
　See CHILL.

THE MAX
　The height of something; the supreme state of something;
　the ultimate. This meaning has crossed over. See also DO IT
　TO THE MAX.

MAY LIKE
　To pretend something is true when it isn't. "She may like
　she was sick, but she wadn't." AAE pronunciation of
　"make/made like."

MC
　The Rapper; literally, the "Master of Ceremonies." In RAP,
　the *MC*, not the DJ, does the RAPpin.

ME AND YOU
　Used as a challenge to fight ONE-ON-ONE, HEAD-UP.

MEAN
　See DEF.

MECCA
　Harlem, in the vocabulary of the FIVE PERCENT NA-
　TION.

MELLOW
　A very close friend.

MEMBER
　Any African American; derived from the notion of racial
　bonding and solidarity of Blacks.

MESS
　Nonsense; a bunch of crap; bullshit.

MESS AROUND
　1) To take it slow, hang around, do nothing important. This

....

use has crossed over. 2) To have an affair outside one's monogamous relationship. Also *play*. This use has not crossed
over.

MESS WITH

To bother someone; to hassle or irritate a person. Crossover
expression.

MESS WITH SOMEONE'S MIND

To confuse someone through mental gymnastics; to un-
nerve or rattle a person emotionally or psychologically.

MF

Euphemism for MUTHAFUCKA.

MICHAEL WHITE JACKSON

The entertainer Michael Jackson; a reference to the ever-in-
creasing lightening ("whitening") of his natural skin color,
along with a perception of his rejection of African features,
coinciding with plastic surgery on his nose and face creating a more European physical look. This view persists despite Michael's recent revelation that he has the skin disorder vitiligo.

MICKEY D

Any McDonald's restaurant.

MICKEY MOUSE

Petty, unimportant, small-time. Crossover term.

MICKEY MOUSE IS IN THE HOUSE, AND DONALD DUCK
DON'T GIVE A FUCK!

An expression used at parties to suggest, Let's take the
party to a higher level; let's party with abandon, drop all serious concerns, stressors, and the burdens of daily life.

MICKEY T

A woman who goes after men for their wealth and power.

MIDNIGHT HOUR

1) A Traditional Black Church reference to a time when a
person is in search of answers through prayer, deep medita-

tion, and reflection, usually late at night when the person is alone. 2) By extension, any low point in one's life, a period of depression when things have gone wrong and one is in search of solutions.

MIND'S EYE

The inner "eye" of the brain as the source of insight and foresight. Intuition, or the intuitive faculty, is believed to exist in all people, but spiritually developed, wise people are thought to have more acute "vision" in their *mind's eye.* Probably derived from Kemetic philosophy/Egyptology, once highly popular in the Black community and resurfacing today.

MISS ANN

See ANN.

MISS THANG

1) An arrogant woman, one who acts high and mighty. 2) A derogatory term for a gay male who, through dress and behavior, over-exaggerates his femaleness.

MISSION

See ON A MISSION.

MISTA CHARLIE

See CHARLIE.

MISTA FRANKLIN

Euphemism for MUTHAFUCKA.

MISTA WIND

See HAWK.

MOANUHS' BENCH

A special pew set aside during a Traditional Black Church revival—an annual week-long program of nightly sermons, Gospel singing, feasting, and praying aimed at acquiring new converts. The unSAVED who wish to seek salvation sit in this special pew in order to receive special attention from the AMEN CORNER, the choir, the preacher, and others trying to bring on the Spirit. On this symbolic *bench*, the unsaved mourn (*moan*) their sinful, unrepentant state. "Mourners'" is pronounced as *moanuhs'* in AAE; see Introduction.

MOJO

Originally, a magical charm. By extension, a source of personal magic that one can tap into, enabling you to work magic on something or to put somebody under your spell. "You got yo mojo workin, but it ain gon work on me!" Derived from *moco'o*, literally, "medicine man," in the Fula language of West Africa.

MOLDED

Old.

MOMMA

A form of address for a woman, used by males and females, especially for a woman who is DOWN.

MONDO

Large; extremely big.

MONEY

A form of address for any male, as in "Yo, Money! Sup?" Also *G* (newer term); *man, Jack, Bo-jack, Bo-dick* (older terms).

MONSTA

See DEF.

MORE COAL ON THE FIRE

Used by women in reference to a sexually inept man, as in "Put more coal on the fire" or "You need more coal on the fire."

MORINEY (PRONOUNCED MUH-RHINE-EE)

Describes an African American who has a light complexion with reddish tones to the skin.

MOTHER

1) A title and form of address for older women in the Traditional Black Church. 2) Euphemism for MUTHAFUCKA.

MOTHER HUBBARD
Euphemism for MUTHAFUCKA.

MOTHER WIT
Common sense, intuition; wisdom not taught in school or found in books.

MOTHERLODE
The core, the center, the main thing.

MOTHER'S DAY
The day women on welfare/ADC get their checks.

MOTHER'S DAY PIMP
A man who lives off—PIMPS off—women on welfare/ ADC, and who collects their checks on MOTHER'S DAY.

MOTHERSHIP
1) See MOTHERLODE. 2) The lead car in an automobile caravan.

MOTOR
See JET (newer term).

MOTOR CITY
Detroit. Crossover term. See also D.

MOTOWN
1) Detroit. Crossover term. See also D. 2) The sound or style of music that originated in Detroit in the 1960s and spread around the world.

MOURNERS' BENCH
See MOANUHS' BENCH.

MOUTHPIECE
Gold caps on the front teeth. Also *front, gold front.*

MUG
Euphemism for MUTHAFUCKA.

MUH-FUH
See MUTHAFUCKA.

MURDER MOUTH
To make wild, outlandish threats that you don't have the power or guts to execute. See also FAT MOUTH.

MURPHY

A scam or con game played on white men, usually involving sex for hire.

MUTHAFUCKA

Used to refer to a person, place, or thing, either negatively or positively, depending on the context. It *never* refers to a person who has sex with his/her mother. "Now that's a bad muthafucka," meaning, That's a beautiful car; "Michael Jordan is a muthafucka on the court," meaning, Michael Jordan's basketball-playing prowess is extraordinary; "That Joadie, now he is one sorry muthafucka," i.e., The man in question is a rather useless, good-for-nothing person. Also used for emphasis: "You muthafuckin right I wadn't goin," that is, You are exactly correct in thinking that I wasn't going.

THE N-WORD

Euphemism for NIGGER and NIGGA.

NAP UP

What STRAIGHTENed hair does when it returns to its original, tightly curled (KINKY, NAPPY) state.

NAPPY

See KINKY.

NAPS

See KINKS.

THE NATION

The Nation of Islam, a Black Muslim group, today under the leadership of Minister Louis Farrakhan. Founded in 1930 by W. D. Fard; led by Elijah Muhammad for decades; the chief spokesperson in the 1960s was Malcolm X.

Stresses clean living, self-help, respect for women, and African-Centered knowledge. Applauded for resurrection of drug addicts, criminals, and street people—especially males. Minister Farrakhan enjoys a strong following among Black youth, and in a national poll of adult Blacks, 70 percent thought he said things the country should hear and 62 percent felt he was good for the COMMUNITY (*Time* magazine, February 28, 1994). The religious theology is similar to, but with some adaptations from, the older, traditional Islamic faith.

THE NATION

A generic name for a gang.

NATURAL

African American hair worn in its natural state, not HOT-COMBed or treated with chemical straighteners.

NATURAL HIGH

A state of excitement or exuberance induced by inner, spiritual forces; a BUZZ not due to liquor or drugs.

NATURE

A generic reference to a person's sex drive; one's libido. See also a LOT OF NATURE, NO NATURE.

NEARER, MY GOD, TO THEE

See GOOD HAIR.

NECK

See RED NECK.

NEGRO

A person of African descent; the term originally was not capitalized. From about 1930 to the 1960s, the preferred term among intellectuals and the middle class. However, many working-class Negroes never were quite comfortable with *Negro,* possibly because of the way it was often pronounced—"nigra," making it sound close to NIGGER. The term fell into disfavor during the Black Freedom Struggle of the 1960s and 1970s, and has come to be used for

African Americans opposed to Black causes and/or those who identify with European Americans. See Introduction.

NEO-SLAVERY

Used by AFRICAN-CENTERED and activist people to refer to the current state of African America: nothing has changed (or the more things change, the more they remain the same). The current condition of Blacks is viewed as simply a movement from legal slavery to a new form of enslavement, since Blacks are still powerless and whites powerful, as in the enslavement era. The term also links the African American situation to that of post-independence Africans who merely moved from colonization to neo-colonization.

NEW JACK

1) The new urban HIP HOP Culture. 2) In tune or in sync with the HOOD. 3) Culturally upscale.

NEW JILL

The female version of urban HIP HOP Culture. Conveys a new female assertiveness, branching out from NEW JACK and establishing the SISTAS' own thang.

NICE

High, usually on drugs or liquor.

NICKEL

1) Five dollars. 2) A quantity of marijuana selling for five dollars (a *nickel* BAG). Crossover meaning.

NICKEL N DIME

Refers to a small-time, petty idea, person, or event. "It ain nothin but a nickel n dime operation"; "I don't like for people to nickel n dime me." Crossover expression.

NICKEL SLICK

Petty, small-time; refers to a low-level attempt to manipulate people or situations; trying to be SLICK but falling short. "That nickel slick shit you pulled didn work, did it?"

NIGGA

Used with a variety of meanings, ranging from positive to negative to neutral. 1) "She my main nigga," that is, She is my close friend, my back-up. 2) "Now that Brotha, see, he ain like them ol e-lights, he real, he is a shonuff nigga," i.e., He is culturally Black and rooted in Blackness and the African American Experience. 3) "That party was live; it was wall-to-wall niggas there," a generic, neutral use of the word, meaning simply that many African Americans were present at the party. 4) "Guess we ain gon be seein too much of girlfriend no mo since she got herself a new nigga," African American women's neutral/generic term for a Black man, here meaning simply that the woman in question has a new boyfriend. 5) *The Source* magazine, describing filmmaker Spike Lee and NBA (Phoenix Suns) superstar Charles Barkley: "Nineties Niggers . . . two outspoken Black men. . . . Charles calls the ones that push and fight '90's Niggers.'" While with the Philadelphia 76ers, Barkley answered the press about a bad shot he had made: "I'm a 90's nigger. . . . *The Daily News, The Inquirer* has been on my back. . . . They want their Black athletes to be Uncle Toms. I told you white boys you've never heard of a 90's nigger. We do what we want to do" (*The Source*, December 1992). *Nigga* here refers to a rebellious, fearless, unconventional, IN-YA-FACE Black man. 6) "A group of Brothas was buggin out, drinkin the forty ounce, goin the nigga route," a clearly negative use of the word, meaning, Some Black males were on the street, partying, getting drunk off malt liquor, and acting out the loud, vulgar stereotype of a *nigga*, "disrespecting" the BROTHA's "Black Queen, holding their crotches and being obscene" (from RAP group Arrested Development's "People Everyday").

When used by whites, *nigga* has historically been used in a negative sense, as a racial epithet, to CALL an African person OUTA THEY NAME—and usually pronounced "nigger," not *nigga*. However, the frequent use of *nigga* in Rap Music, on "Def Comedy Jam," and throughout Black Culture generally, where the word takes on meanings other than the historical negative, has created a linguistic dilemma in the crossover world and in the African American community. Widespread controversy rages about the use of *nigga* among Blacks—especially the pervasive public use of the term—and about whether or not whites can have license to use THE N-WORD with the many different meanings that Blacks give to it.

We may see greater usage of the emerging term WIGGA / WIGGER, literally, a white *nigga,* in the HIP HOP sense, that is, a European American who strongly identifies with African American Culture—e.g., baggy jeans, gear styled by Cross Colours, and into Spike Lee films, "Def Comedy Jam," and Rapper Ice-T. According to journalist Robin D. Givhan, wiggers "don't just appreciate Black Culture, they have absorbed it. They consider Black Culture their culture. . . . Wiggers have turned stereotypes upside down. They've taken a racial epithet, reworked it and come up with a word that is not an insult, just a description" (*Detroit Free Press,* June 21, 1993). See also BAD NIGGA, FIELD NIGGA, HOUSE NIGGA.

NIGGA MESS

Any messy personal or community affair of African Americans; something that should be resolved in-house, within the COMMUNITY or Black "family."

NIGGA-TOE

A type of nut, known as a Brazil nut. Because of the word *nigga,* the term may cause offense.

NIGGAMATION

Used in reference to the practice of speedups on automobile and other industrial assembly lines, where the majority of the workers are African American, in order to increase productivity without having to pay workers overtime wages. This once-widespread practice often led to serious injuries among Black production workers, who charged that the industrial corporations increased productivity by exploiting Black labor, not by using automation—thus *niggamation*.

NIGGER
See NIGGA.

NINE
A nine-millimeter semi-automatic gun; can be purchased legally, but sold on the street for $500–$1,000. See also the WHOLE NINE.

NIP
A small quantity of liquor; possibly derived from the *nipple* of a baby's milk bottle.

NITTY GRITTY
The core, fundamental essence of something. Crossover term.

N.O.
New Orleans.

NO COUNT
1) Of insufficient quality or durability; useless. "That chair he bought ain no count." 2) Describes a person who is not of any help. "When it's time to work, he ain no count."

NO LONGER THAN JOHN STAYED IN THE ARMY
A very short period of time.

NO NATURE
Describes a person who has a very low sex drive.

NOD
1) Sleep. "I think I'll cop a nod." 2) A state of semiconsciousness induced by heroin.

NOISE
Music, particularly instrumental music rather than vocals.

See also Bring/Brang the noise!, Shut the noise!

NONE

No sex; used by males or females. "She wouldn give me none"; "He ain givin me none, but I got a Plan B." See also some.

NONE-YUH

None of your business; stop dippin.

NOOKIE

Euphemism for pussy.

NOSE JOB

A person who is hopelessly in love and vulnerable is said to have received a *nose job*. Also got his/her nose, got his/her nose open.

NOSE OPEN

See got his/her nose open.

NOT TRYIN TA

An expression used to dismiss what somebody is saying, to disregard an option or course of action that the person is proposing; in short, "I'm not even listening."

N's

Money. Possibly from "notes," i.e., the bank notes of paper currency. Also *scratch*. *Scratch* has crossed over, but *N's* has not.

NUMBER GAME

See Numbers.

NUMBER MAN

See Numbers.

NUMBER ONE

Urination. Crossover term.

NUMBER TWO

1) Bowel movement. Crossover use. 2) Something rank, wrong, deceptive, unethical, or immoral, in the sense of shit. This use has not crossed over. "Many of these elected

officials are full of number two"; "Liberals [white liberals] will give you a whole lot of number two if you don't watch them."

NUMBERS

A once highly popular illegal betting game, played in communities across the nation; similar to today's state lotteries. Betting was referred to as PLAYing THE NUMBERS. An entire culture, employment industry, and lexicon developed around the *Numbers*. Many *Number men* (chiefs who *backed the Numbers,* i.e., guaranteed and paid off the bets) were respected leaders and business people in the COMMUNITY. With the advent of state lotteries, the community's *Number Game* declined considerably, although it still exists on a smaller scale in many communities today.

NUT

See GIT A NUT.

NUT OUT

To go crazy; to act irrationally.

NUT ROLL

A great deal of money; a big bankroll carried on the person.

NUTS

Testicles. See also BUS ONE'S NUTS.

OD

1) To overdo anything; to do something to excess. "I ODed on the chitlins." 2) To overdose on drugs (older usage). This use has crossed over.

OFAY

A reference to any white person; no longer derogatory, but

originally negative. Probably from Pig Latin for "foe" (enemy) and West African language sources, in words such as *ofaginzy,* literally "white man." Also *fay.*

OFF

To kill somebody.

OG

Original Gangster; a gang member who has earned PROPS because of his bold actions.

OIL

Liquor.

OKAY

All right, "OK." From the form *kay* in several West African languages, meaning "yes," "of course," "indeed" (Wolof *waw Kay/waw Ke,* Mandingo *o-ke,* Fulani *eeyi kay*). Crossover term.

OKE-DOKE (PRONOUNCED OH-KEY-DOHK)

A scam, con, deception. "I ain goin for the oke-doke."

OLD HEAD

An older person; generally suggests the person is not only older but wiser.

OLD SCHOOL

1) The style of RAP Music in its early days, beginning in the 1970s. Exemplified by such Rappers as Grandmaster Flash, The Sugarhill Gang, and Afrika Bambaataa. 2) Anything from the 1960s and 1970s. "Bell-bottom pants, platform shoes, that's Old School." 3) A reference to the status of a seasoned veteran or a person highly experienced in something (older usage); probably derived from African Americans' stress on the significance of life and living as a teacher, the "school" of experience.

ON

See DEF.

ON A MISSION

Staunchly dedicated to achieving an objective.

ON E
> Empty, lacking something; generally, but not necessarily, used to refer to being out of money. Derived from the "E" on the gas gauge of a vehicle.

ON FULL
> Having plenty of something; generally, but not necessarily, used in reference to having plenty of money — "plenty" being whatever an individual considers it to be.

ON IT
> In control; on top of a situation.

ON IT LIKE A HONET
> Very much in control and on top of a situation. "Hornet" rendered as *honet* in AAE; see Introduction.

ON OVERRIDE
> Describes the fact that a person remains quiet and low-key, displays no reaction to an explosive or emotional situation, or maintains his or her COOL in the face of a DIS or other negative statement or action. Older use of the term possibly derived from the function of the "overdrive" in older cars, which was used to drown out or "override" engine noise, keeping it quiet. Current use possibly derives from "override" in computer technology, referring to the act of bypassing a program, utility, or computer instruction that is in place in order to perform some other operation desired by the user.

ON SOMEBODY'S CASE
> Nagging or harassing a person about a situation or matter. "My momma is on my case about school," that is, She is fussing at me about my situation at school. This use has crossed over. See also CASE, GIT OFF MY CASE.

ON SOMEBODY'S SHIT LIST
> Indicates anger at or disapproval of a person; relegating that individual to the group (*list*) of people who are out of favor with someone.

ON T
  See ON TIME/ON T.

ON THE BLOCK
  Used to refer to a prostitute who works the streets.

ON THE CASE
  Taking care of business; on top of a situation. "When I
  need my taxes done, I go to boyfriend cause he be on the
  case."

ON THE FLY
  Living or acting in a dazzling, ultra-hip manner.

ON THE OUTS
  1) Angry or feuding with somebody. 2) Released from
  prison.

ON THE PIPE
  1) Addicted to crack. 2) The act of FREEBASin cocaine.

ON THE RAG
  Menstruating. Crossover expression.

ON THE STRENGTH
  An expression used to reinforce or reaffirm the seriousness
  of something; indicates something that is noteworthy. Probably a resurfacing and variation of STRONG.

ON TIME/ON T
  At the appropriate natural, psychological moment, regard-
  less of "clock" time. Probably from the Traditional Black
  Church expression associated with the story of Job. "He
  [God] may not come when you want Him, but He's right
  on time."

ONE-EIGHT-SEVEN (1-8-7)
  To murder somebody.

ONE-ON-ONE
  1) Refers to a popular style of playing basketball involving
  only two players. 2) By extension, used in reference to any
  hard, HEAD-UP competition or confrontation between just
  two individuals.

ONE TIME
   1) Exactly, that's right on the money. 2) The police, in West
   Coast lingo.

OPB
   Other people's brand (of cigarettes); said in reference to
   somebody's needing a cigarette and having to borrow it and
   smoke whatever brand the other person is smoking.

OPP
   Other people's (sexual) property; originally, other people's
   PUSSY. Used in reference to a person involved in a sexual
   affair with someone else's MAN or WOMAN. A resurfacing
   and extension of OPB.

OPRAH
   To dredge intimate facts from a person. Derived from the
   name of the talk show host Oprah Winfrey, who uses this
   strategy with dramatic effect, getting people to reveal inner-
   most information about their lives on national television.

OREO
   An African American who is Black in skin color but white
   in thinking and attitudes; like the cookie, black on the outside, white on the inside.

OUT BOX
   From the beginning.

OUTA HERE
   Gone; goodbye; I'm leaving. Crossover expression in the
   form "I'm outa here." Also *Outtie 5000* (newer term);
   Later, Catch you later (older expressions).

OUTA SIGHT
   Crossover term. See DEF (newer term).

OUTSIDE KID
   A baby born out of wedlock; "illegitimate" child.

OUTTIE 5000
   I'm gone; goodbye. AAE version of "Audi 5000." Also
   outa here; and Later, Catch you later (older expressions).

OVAH

See GIT OVAH, GIT OVAH ON, GO OVAH.

OVERRIDE

See ON OVERRIDE.

P

P

1) A reference to anything in its pure, unadulterated state, such as drugs. 2) Euphemism for PUSSY.

PACKER'S CLUB

Used in reference to any woman involved with a man unable to maintain an erection during sexual intercourse; such women are said to be "members of the *packer's club*." See also PACKIN CHITLINS.

PACKIN

1) Refers to a person carrying a gun. "Be cool; he's packin." 2) Refers to a man who has a large penis. "Check that out. Is the Brotha packin or what?" 3) What the male does during the sex act.

PACKIN CHITLINS

Used by women to refer to a man whose erection during sex is not hard, or who is unable to maintain an erection. See also PACKER'S CLUB.

PAD

A house. See CRIB.

PADDY

Any white person; a neutral, generic term by now.

PAPER

Money. See also BIG PAPER.

PAPERS

Divorce summons and divorce settlement documents.

PARANOID

 1) Suspicious, anxious, constantly on guard against a racist statement or behavior, or a European American pulling a fast one. 2) Concerned about the possibility of getting killed, especially while in the HOOD. 3) Scared to death; frightened. For African Americans, being *paranoid* is not characteristic of mental imbalance but a survival strategy.

PARLAY!

 Slow it down. As this term settles in, it is moving closer in meaning to CHILL.

PAR-TAY

 A party, pronounced *par-tay* to suggest a lively, high-spirited event, as in "The par-tay was live!" Also *to par-tay*, as in "We got to par-tay tonight, Jack."

PARTNER

 1) One's close friend or associate. 2) One's lover or "significant other."

PARTY

 See PAR-TAY.

PASS[1]

 Euphemism for *died*. "His mother has just pass." AAE pronunciation of "passed"; see Introduction.

PASS[2]

 To pass oneself off as white; to live life as a European American. Obviously only possible for very FAIR Blacks with hair and other physical features that are NEARER, MY GOD, TO THEE.

PAY DUES

 To have it hard in one's life, as if "paying" your "debt" for having had it easy.

PAYBACK

 The return of something negative to the person who initiated the negativity, reaffirming Blacks' belief in the philosophy WHAT GO ROUND COME ROUND.

PCP

Phencyclidine, an animal tranquilizer, used as an illegal
street drug; induces a psychedelic effect. Also *angel dust.*

PEACE

Goodbye. Popularized by the FIVE PERCENT NATION.
Also *Peace out.*

PEACE OUT

See PEACE.

PEANUT BUTTER

Anal sex.

PECK

See PECKAWOOD.

PECKAWOOD

1) Any white person. 2) A lower-class white person. A derogatory term. "Peckerwood" rendered in AAE pronunciation; see Introduction. Also *peck, wood.*

PEEL A CAP

See BUS A CAP.

PEEP

1) To discover someone or something that one wasn't ex-
pected to. 2) To observe someone or something.

PEEP THINGS OUT

To see what's going on.

PEOPLE OF COLOR

Generic term for BLACKS, Chicanos/Hispanics/Latinos,
Asians, Native Americans/Indians, and other "non-white"
peoples, especially in the United States, but also around the
globe. See also COLORED PEOPLE.

PERM

Refers to the process of STRAIGHTENing hair using chemi-
cals, as well as to the resulting hairdo. The natural tight
curl is RELAXed, and a straight style or less tightly curled
style is imposed onto the natural hair. From "permanent."

PERP

Perpetrator; one who is pretending, faking it.

PERPETRATIN

Acting like something you're not; pretending, faking, FRONTing. Also *perpin.*

PERPETRATOR

See PERP.

PERPIN

See PERPETRATIN.

PHAT

See DEF. Probably derived from "em-PHAT-ically"; also a play on the word "fat" (see Introduction).

PHILLY

A cheap cigar used for smoking crack. Also *Philly blunt.*

PHILLY / PHILADELPHIA BANKROLL

A lot of one-dollar bills wrapped underneath a hundred-dollar bill to make it appear that a person has a lot of money.

PHILLY BLUNT

See PHILLY.

PICK-UP GAME

In basketball, an informal or impromptu game, with players not known to one another or who do not generally play

mission of the artist, Craig Rex Perry, and *Young Sisters and Brothers Magazine.*

together; very popular on the outdoor ("official" or "home-made") courts of urban areas.

PICK-UP LADY / MAN

A person who collects the NUMBERS bets in the community and turns them in to the NUMBER MAN (the man BACKING THE NUMBERS). The winning combination is made up of three digits, but it is possible to bet on only one digit. If the *pick-up lady/man* collects bets on one digit only, she/he is referred to as a *single action lady/man*.

PICTURE

A movie. "Did y'all see the picture wit my girl, Janet, in it yet?" (a reference to Janet Jackson in John Singleton's 1993 film *Poetic Justice*).

PIECE

1) Sex with a woman; euphemism for PUSSY. See also STRAY PIECE. 2) A gun. This meaning has crossed over.

PIG LATIN

A coded form of English in the Black Verbal Tradition. Once very popular, but now fading. To speak it, move the first letter of a word to the end of the word and add *ay*. Thus *boy = oybay; girl = irlgay; foe = ofay*. If a word begins with two consonant sounds, then shift both letters. Thus *store = orestay; Black = ackblay*. Although not heard as frequently today among youth as in the previous generation, middle-aged Blacks occasionally use *Pig Latin,* especially some women who incorporate and code "cuss" words this way in their informal speaking style. For example, a prominent African American woman college administrator recently said to a small group of women: "You see, Sistas, I let the good white folk know in my own way that I was not going to take their *itshay*."

PILL

A basketball.

PIMP[1]

1) A man who lives off the earnings of a prostitute; not to be confused with the pimp as a procurer or solicitor. This meaning of *pimp* is one who "rest, dress, and request." 2) A man or woman who lives off the earnings of another person in an exploitative relationship.

PIMP[2]

1) To exploit someone or something. "He's pimpin religion," that is, He is using the church as a front for some kind of personal gain, such as money, popularity, political advantage, etc. 2) To dominate one's competition in sports.

PIMP SLAP

An open-handed slap across the face.

PIMP STRUT

See GANGSTA LIMP.

PIMP WALK

See GANGSTA LIMP.

PIMPED OUT

Well-dressed.

PINK TOES

A reference to a white woman; the color pink suggesting softness, delicateness, and tenderness, reflecting the stereotype of the soft, tender, delicate quality of the white woman's body.

PIPE

See LAY PIPE, ON THE PIPE.

PITCH A BITCH

To complain; to create conflict through loud, confrontational, argumentative talk.

PLAY

1) To be involved in affairs outside one's main relationship. 2) To deceive someone; to put something over on a person, to outsmart them. "We all got played" is how a BROTHA

characterized the split decision in the Federal trial of the police officers involved in the Rodney King beating in Los Angeles (two officers found guilty; two acquitted).

PLAY OUT

1) To lose value, usefulness, or effectiveness; also, to lose the attraction or interest of someone; can be used with reference to a thing or a person. "This little machine is bout to play out." (The speaker is talking about her answering machine, which is no longer working properly.) "My man was in there for a minute, but he done played out now." (The speaker is referring to a male friend of his who has lost his WOMAN's interest.) Also *run out.* 2) To become outdated. This meaning has crossed over.

PLAY PAST

To miss an opportunity, usually because you were unprepared or your business/GAME wasn't TOGETHA. "I think the man was gon offer the Brotha the job, but the Brotha kept goin on about some dumb shit and played right past it."

PLAY PUSSY AND GIT FUCKED

Used as a warning or threat; if you present a PUSSY, you can expect it to be fucked. That is, if you do or say a certain thing, be prepared to suffer the consequences.

PLAY SOME BID

See BID.

PLAY SOMEBODY CLOSE

To test a person's will, seeing how far you can go in trying to manipulate the person before getting caught.

PLAY SOMEBODY FOR HIS/HER REACTION

To say something to test out how a person reacts to it.

PLAY SOMETHING OFF

To avoid confrontation or having to deal with or talk about something by diverting attention to something else.

PLAY THAT

Used in the negative, "I don't play that," meaning, I don't like what you said or did, or are about to say or do, and I will not accept it.

PLAY THE DOZENS

See the DOZENS.

PLAY THE NUMBERS

To place a bet on the number one believes will FALL OUT. See also NUMBERS.

PLAYER

1) A man or woman who has many women or men and PLAYS them. 2) A flamboyant, flashy, popular man or woman, who may or may not have many women or men in his or her life.

PLAYIN FOR BLOOD

Used in reference to serious, aggressive, hard play in cards, basketball, Nintendo, or any other competitive activity, such as a debate, an argument, etc.

PLUCK

Wine. Possibly derived from *pluck,* meaning "courage"; in earlier years, wine was often drunk before gang fights. Today's *pluck* is the FORTY.

PO-LICE

The police, AAE pronunciation; see Introduction.

POONTANG

Euphemism for PUSSY.

POOT

To pass gas.

POOT-BUTT

1) A small-time, unimportant person. 2) Someone who isn't motivated to strive or work toward a goal.

POOTENANNY

Euphemism for PUSSY.

POP

1) To shoot someone. 2) To steal. 3) To have sex.

POP A CAP

See BUS A CAP.

POP A CAR

To steal a car.

POP SOMEBODY

To deceive, lie, manipulate, GIT OVAH ON a person.

POSSE

Associates, friends; one's social group. Also *crew, clique.*

POUNDIN

1) Drinking large amounts of liquor rapidly. 2) A male performing very hard, vigorous sex is said to be *poundin.*

PP

Personal problem; used to dismiss or discount a person's
complaint about something.

PRESS

To STRAIGHTEN the hair by using a HOT COMB.

PRIMO

1) Excellent, high-quality, powerful marijuana. 2) See
FIFTY-ONE.

PROCESS

See CONK.

PROFILE

To assume a pose of confidence and COOLNESS. See also
STYLIN AND PROFILIN.

PROGRAM

1) A verbal strategy, a scheme or plan of verbal action for
handling any situation. "Girlfriend working her program."
Similar to GAME, in the sense of a story or RAP used to obtain a desired end. However, runnin a *program* can be positive or negative, whereas runnin a *game* is deceptive and
manipulative. 2) The established routine or pattern of

something—an organization, an event, an activity, etc. "Yo, git wit the program, baby!" (said to a member of an aerobics class who has slowed down during an exercise session). 3) The way you operate, your life style, your way of doing things. "Any dude that ain wit my program can go right back where he came from cause I'm not havin it."

PROMISED LAND

Any place north of the Mason-Dixon Line. The failure of Reconstruction ended the "freedmen's" dream of equity and first-class citizenship in the South. The death of Reconstruction was symbolized by the 1877 compromise that elected Rutherford B. Hayes to the presidency, the politicians' agreement to return home rule to the Confederates, and the withdrawal of Federal troops from the South. From 1877 until the 1960s Freedom Struggle, African Americans believed that the northern United States was free of segregation and racism. Thus, like the Hebrews in the Old Testament, they "escaped" in massive numbers out of "Egypt" (the Jim Crow South), fleeing to the "Promised Land" (the North). The explosion of this myth was given literary voice in *Manchild in the Promised Land* (1965), a hot-selling autobiography by Claude Brown.

PROPERS

1) Respect. 2) Recognition for doing or saying something. Also *props* (newer term).

PROPS

See PROPERS (older term).

PSYCH / PSYCH OUT

1) To use clever deception to persuade a person to think or act the way you want him/her to. 2) To fake out or fool someone using one's mental powers.

PUFFER

See CRACKHEAD.

PULL A TRAIN

Refers to several males having sex with one female at the same time. Also *run a train*.

PULL SHIT

To do something low-down, treacherous, and mean to someone.

PULL SOMEONE'S COAT

To enlighten someone; to HIP a person to something.

PUMP IT UP!

1) See BRING/BRANG THE NOISE! 2) By extension, to intensify anything; to up the energy and power level of something. Also *Pump up the volume!*

PUMP UP THE VOLUME!

See BRING/BRANG THE NOISE!, PUMP IT UP!

PUMPIN

See DEF.

PUNK

1) A cowardly, passive person; a nonfighter. 2) A gay man (derogatory reference). 3) Someone who backs down, knuckles under to a stronger, more aggressive force. See also PUNK OUT.

PUNK OUT

To turn someone into a passive person who knuckles under and backs down from his or her position.

PUSH UP ON

1) See HIT ON (older term); GIT WIT (newer term). 2) To make romantic moves on a person for sex. 3) To intimidate someone.

PUSSY

1) Sex from a female. 2) The vagina.

PUSSY-WHUPPED

Refers to a man who lets his WOMAN boss him around because of her sexual power over him. Crossover term. The female version is DICK-WHUPPED, which has not crossed over.

PUT A BABY ON A MAN
1) To have a child without the father's knowledge and/or consent. 2) To claim as the father of your child a man who is not the father.

PUT ON WAX
See WAX[1].

PUT OUT WITH SOMEBODY OR SOMETHING
Annoyed or exasperated with someone, something, or an event, to the point of no longer associating with the person or thing or participating in the event.

PUT SHIT ON SOMEBODY
To take advantage of somebody; to manipulate or con a person.

PUT SOMEBODY IN CHECK
See CHECK.

PUT SOMEBODY ON FRONT STREET
See FRONT[2].

PUT SOMEBODY'S BIDNESS IN THE STREET
To make public someone's personal affairs, personal experience, or some aspect of their personal situation by openly discussing it with others.

PUT THE IG ON
To DIS somebody by applying the *ig*, that is, by refusing to acknowledge their presence or ignoring them. See also IG.

Q

Q
    Barbecued ribs.

QUICK, FAST, AND IN A HURRY
Refers to doing or understanding something extremely fast.

QUIET AS IT'S KEPT
Here's the little-known truth about something.

QUO VADIS
A male hairstyle, cut short and combed to the front; popular from the 1950s to about the mid-1960s and the advent of the NATURAL hairstyle. Probably derived from the 1951 film epic *Quo Vadis,* set in Rome thirty years after the death of Jesus Christ. *Quo Vadis, The Robe,* and other big-screen historical religious epics of this era portrayed Christians and Romans, some wearing this hairstyle. Also *caesar.*

RACE MAN / WOMAN
A person who is devoted to, DOWN FOR the race, promotes African American Culture, and staunchly defends Blacks; for example, Dr. Carter G. Woodson, founder of today's Black History Month in 1926 (then it was "Negro History Week"). The concept and term both date back to the early 1900s, when being a *race man* or *woman* was a full-time preoccupation, engaged in by self-conscious Blacks who worked ordinary jobs for survival and took on racial promotion activities, usually for no monetary benefit or personal gain. Other *race men* of this era were Marcus Garvey, J. A. Rogers, W. E. B. DuBois, and Monroe Trotter. A significant *race woman* of the time was Ida B. Wells, who risked her life to conduct extensive investigations into the lynchings of Black men. *Race men* and *women* in the 1990s include people like Sister Dr. Johnetta Cole, president of

Spelman College, and Dr. Henry Louis Gates, of Harvard University (who in a 1990 *New York Times* cover story described himself as a *race man*); HIP HOP *race men* and *women* are folk such as Public Enemy, Paris, Arrested Development, Queen Latifah, Ice Cube, and Ice-T (sometimes).

RADA

An Eldorado Cadillac, once a very popular status symbol among PLAYERS, preachers, and the FLY.

RAG[1]

A gang member.

RAG[2]

1) To DIS someone. 2) To criticize a person harshly. 3) To make fun of someone.

RAGAMUFFIN

A down-to-earth person. Probably from the Jamaican style of music that combines RAP and reggae to convey messages about ordinary people, their problems, and their politics.

RAGAMUFFIN TIP

An ordinary, down-to-earth status or situation. See also TIP[1].

RAGGEDY

Not up to par; unHIP, uncOOL. "Yo shit is raggedy," that is, In this area of life (whatever it happens to be), your behavior or BIDNESS is dysfunctional and ineffective.

RAGS

Stylish clothes.

RAISE

To leave.

RAISE CAIN

See RAISE SAND, the more common expression in the COMMUNITY. *Raise Cain* derives from the Old Testament story of Cain, Adam and Eve's son, who murdered his brother Abel and was banished from the community. To "raise Cain" is to make enough noise or fuss to raise up Cain.

RAISE SAND

To talk loud, engage in provocative, argumentative behavior. Also *raise Cain*.

RANK[1]

To downgrade something or someone. Also *low rate*.

RANK[2]

In bad taste.

RAP

Musical style rooted in the Black Verbal Tradition—talk-singing, SIGNIFYIN, blending reality and fiction. A contemporary Black response to conditions of joblessness, poverty, and disempowerment; a rebellion against what a cultural critic from the "front lines of the White Struggle" calls "white America's economic and psychological terrorism against Black people—reduced in the white mind to 'prejudice' and 'stereotypes,' concepts more within its cultural experience" (Upski, "We Use Words Like 'Mackadocious,'" *The Source,* May 1993).

RAP[1]

Originally, *rap* referred only to romantic conversation from a man to a woman to win her affection and sexual favors. When the term crossed over, it lost its sexual flavor and has come to mean any kind of strong, aggressive, highly fluent, powerful talk.

RAP[2]

1) To talk in a romantic style to win over a woman, especially sexually. 2) To talk in a strong, aggressive style on any subject. Crossover meaning.

RAP ATTACK

1) Listening to a lot of RAP Music at one time. 2) Nonstop,

strong, aggressive talk; can't stop RAPpin.

RASPBERRY

A male who sells himself to other men for drugs or money
to buy drugs. A female who does the same is a STRAW-
BERRY.

RASTA

A follower of RASTAFARIA.

RASTAFARIA

A cultural and religious movement of resistance to enslavement in the early years and to white racism and domination
after emancipation. Originated in Jamaica; its spiritual base
is the Ethiopianism of Haile Selassie, whose former name
was Ras (in the Amharic language, "prince") Tafari (Amharic, "to be feared"). *Rastafarians* have often been misunderstood because of their cultural practices—wearing
DREADLOCKS, smoking GANJA/the Chillum Pipe, and
their strong, rebellious reggae music. Yet RASTA men such
as the late Bob Marley promoted the drum as a tool of communication with working-class Jamaicans and other Africans in the Caribbean and used reggae for social and political commentary. "The Rastafari has dramatised the
question that has always been uncomfortable in Caribbean
history, and the question is where you stand in relation to
blackness" (George Lamming, quoted in *Rasta and Resistance*, 1987).

RASTAFARIAN

See RASTAFARIA.

RAT PACK

A group that gangs up to beat somebody up.

RAW

1) Refers to the actual truth or status of something, the
"real deal." 2) See DEF. 3) Refers to having sex without a
condom. 4) Describes cocaine without any additives.

READ

To tell someone off in no uncertain terms and in a verbally elaborate manner. See also TAKE A TEXT.

READY

Excellent, superb, great. "The catfish was ready."

REBELLION

A term used by activists and AFRICAN-CENTERED folk to describe a mass display of dissatisfaction with the system. *Rebellions* have occurred throughout African American history, for instance, during the 1960s and 1970s and in South Central Los Angeles in 1992 following the trial of the police officers who brutalized Rodney King. The social disruption and upheaval are perceived as manifestations of a people in struggle, in contrast to the perception of European Americans and the media, who refer to these uprisings as "riots."

RECRUITING

Refers to males on the lookout for females, especially attractive ones.

RED, BLACK, AND GREEN

A color combination suggesting strong identification with Blackness and the Black Experience. "What red, black and green Afrikan B-boy wouldn't want to go over to this twentysomething, Brooklyn flygirl's crib?" (Louis Romain, "A Rose Grows in Brooklyn" [interview with Rosie Perez], *The Source*, July 1993). Derived from the colors of the flag of the "Black Nation," red for blood, black for the people, and green for the land. One of the first proponents of the idea of African Americans as a separate nation was Marcus Garvey (1887–1940), founder and leader of the Universal Negro Improvement Association and of the first mass "Back-to-Africa" movement.

RED EYE

A long, hard stare, usually directed at a person.

RED NECK
Any white person; also, a lower-class white person; a derogatory term. Also *neck*.

REEFER
Marijuana. Crossover term.

RELAXED
Refers to hair that has been STRAIGHTENed using a RELAXER, a chemical treatment that *relaxes* the hair from its natural, tightly curled state, creating either a totally straight look or a loosely curled style, such as the JHERI-CURL. Before the 1970s, females used the HOT COMB method and males used the CONK method to straighten their hair.

RELAXER
See RELAXED.

RENT-A-NIGGA
A derogatory reference to private security guards in COMMUNITY stores and shops, who sometimes insult the Black shoppers and treat them with brutal disrespect. Although perceived as modern-day overseers protecting the white man's property, many guards, who are very often males, indicate that they are desperate and driven to seek this kind of work because no other jobs are available.

REP
A reputation for being powerful or highly accomplished in a field.

RE-UP
To replenish a crack supply for the purpose of ROLLIN.

RIDE¹
1) A car. 2) One's transportation to any place.

RIDE²
To have sex; from the male viewpoint, to *ride* a woman, or from the female viewpoint, to "mount" and *ride* the penis.

RIDE DOWN ON

1) To track somebody down in your vehicle in order to confront the person. 2) In gang terms, to travel by vehicle to a rival gang's territory in order to confront or attack them.

RIDE ON

See RIDE DOWN ON.

RIDE SHOTGUN

To ride in the front passenger seat of a vehicle. From the Wild West practice of having a guard armed with a shotgun ride beside the driver of a stagecoach, which usually transported money as well as people.

RIGHT HAND OF FELLOWSHIP

The extending of a handshake to new or newly converted members of the Traditional Black Church congregation; the ritual involves the entire congregation shaking hands with the new members. The various Black Power handshakes used as greetings in the 1960s and 1970s derived from this ritual. See also SOUL SHAKE.

RIGHT ON T

Right on time. SEE ON TIME/ON T. The response "Right on!" was derived from *right on T* and popularized by the Black Panthers in the 1960s and 1970s.

RIGHTEOUS

Excellent, especially referring to somebody or something that is on the political and/or social activist TIP. "The BROTHA is righteous."

RINKY DINK

Inadequate, insignificant. Crossover term.

RIP

See JUMPSTREET.

RIP OFF

1) To kill someone. 2) To take unfair advantage of someone. 3) To rob someone of his or her material valuables or ideas. Crossover meaning.

....

RIPPED[1]
>   1) Exceptionally unattractive. 2) Intoxicated from liquor; drunk. Crossover meaning.

RIPPED[2]
>   In basketball, refers to the ball being stolen right out in open court, usually in a face-off between the player dribbling the ball and the player CHECKin him. "He can't handle that rock so good. I ripped him a few times."

RISE
>   See HOPS (newer term).

ROACH
>   A marijuana cigarette butt; often used to roll a new marijuana cigarette or a COCKTAIL. Crossover term.

ROAD DOG
>   A HOMEY who always rides around with you.

ROBO COP
>   A hard-core, rigid, gung-ho type of police officer.

ROCK[1]
>   1) A basketball. 2) Cocaine, with no fillers or additives. Crossover meaning.

ROCK[2]
>   1) To jolt, excite extremely. "I'll rock your world." 2) To play exceptionally LIVE music that will get everybody dancing and *rock the house*.

ROCK N ROLL
>   1) Music, dance, and cultural styles begun by African American musicians in the 1950s. Crossover term and meaning; however, ROCK N ROLL in its original Black meaning referred to sexual activity. 2) To fight. 3) To compete. 4) To leave. Also *roll*.

ROCK STAR
>   See CRACKHEAD.

ROCK THE HOUSE
>   See ROCK[2].

ROLE

In the NUMBERS, refers to an object, event, idea, etc., from a dream or an inspiration that comes to you. The term is always used in combination with another word, as in *dead role, shit role, house role*. Each *role* is symbolized by a number, located in the DREAM BOOK, that one can place a bet on.

ROLL

1) To leave. Also *rock n roll*. 2) To drive a car.

ROLL EM UP

1) To roll marijuana cigarettes. 2) To beat somebody up.

ROLLER

A person who sells crack (and other drugs).

ROLLIN

1) The activity of a ROLLER. Also *dealin* (older term). 2) Describes a person who has a nice car (older usage).

ROULIE

See FIFTY-ONE.

RUG RATS

See CRUMB SNATCHERS. Also *table pimps*.

RUN

Something you have to leave the house and do. "I got to make a run" could refer to a simple errand or to something more major that one has to go and do.

RUN A BOSTON

In the game of BID, to win every round of play; to turn all the books (see TURN A BOOK). Also *Boston*.

RUN A DRAG ON

See DRAG¹.

RUN A TRAIN

See PULL A TRAIN.

RUN AND TELL THAT!

A sarcastic statement reflecting on the tendency of some African Americans to "squeal" to European Americans about

their BROTHAS' and SISTAS' plans. The expression probably dates from enslavement, when traitors within the race
would *run and tell* "Ole Massa"about the slaves' schemes
and plans for escape.

RUN IT DOWN
See BREAK IT DOWN.

RUN ONE'S MOUTH
To talk, usually not about anything important.

RUN OUT
See PLAY OUT. "That group used to sang good, but they
done run out now."

RUN THE STREET
To HANG OUT a lot, partying and "good-timing." See also
IN THE STREET.

RUN WILD
To live an unconventional life, in the fast lane, without any
checks or balances on one's behavior.

RUNNIN
Busy; having to make a lot of RUNS. "I been runnin for the
last hour," meaning, I've been busy; "He got a lot of runnin
to do tomorrow," meaning, He'll be very busy and on the
go tomorrow.

RUNNIN OFF AT THE MOUTH
1) Talking excessively. Crossover meaning. Also *jaw jackin,*
which has not crossed over. 2) Gossiping.

RUSH
To jump on somebody; to beat somebody up.

S

SACK CHASER
See GOLD DIGGER, older mainstream slang term that is

resurfacing in HIP HOP Culture. *Sack chaser* has not crossed over.

SADIDDY

Snooty, uppity-acting; acting like "yo shit don't stank." Also *dichty* (older term).

SALTY

Angry, mad. See also JUMP SALTY.

SAM

A derogatory reference to an African American male, possibly from Sambo in *Little Black Sambo*.

SAPPHIRE

A derogatory reference to a Black woman; from a character named Sapphire in the "Amos 'n' Andy" radio program (and later television sitcom), who was the stereotypical EVIL, loud, complaining, emasculating Black woman.

SATURDAY NIGHT SPECIAL

A gun. Originally any small, easily concealed gun, carried only on weekends when trouble might start at a party or out in the street. Crossover term.

SAVED

Refers to a person who has been rescued from the world of sin and now belongs to a special national community of individuals united in Christ and religious spirit.

SAY WHAT?

A response questioning the validity of what somebody has said. Crossover expression.

SCAG

Low-grade heroin that has been diluted (CUT) with something, such as baking powder.

SCANDALOUS

Describes a ruthless or low-down person.

SCANK

See SKEEZER (newer term).

SCARED OF YOU
> A response celebrating someone's accomplishment, skill, achievement, or verbal adeptness.

SCHOLAR
> Any person with a college education.

SCHOOLED
> Describes a person who has learned a lesson through defeat.

SCHOOLGIRL/SCHOOLBOY
> Any person, of any age, going to school or college.

SCIENCE
> Knowledge, information, true facts.

SCOPE
> 1) To watch closely. 2) To keep tabs on somebody through surveillance.

SCOPE SOMETHING OR SOMEBODY OUT
> To observe something or someone in order to analyze or evaluate it or that person. Crossover expression. Also *check it/this/him/her/etc., out.*

SCOTTY
> Crack (or other drugs, but especially crack); used to show the controlling nature of crack use. "She's in bad shape. Scotty got her." On "Star Trek," Scotty operates the machine that beams Kirk and company up and away. *Scotty* is in control.

SCRATCH
> Money; older term that has crossed over. Also *N's,* which has not crossed over.

SCREAM ON
> To put someone down; to DIS a person.

SEEDS
> One's children; rarely used in the singular.

SELL A WOLF TICKET
> See WOOF TICKET.

SELL A WOOF TICKET
See WOOF TICKET.

SELL OUT
1) See CHOKE. 2) To abandon a cause, idea, or style of doing something, usually for personal gain.

SELL-OUT
1) An African American who isn't DOWN WITH the Black
cause, one who betrays the race and compromises the
COMMUNITY's principles, usually for personal gain. Also
sell-out Negro. 2) By extension, anyone who GOES FOR
SELF and abandons his or her group's collective mission.
This meaning has crossed over.

SELL-OUT NEGRO
See SELL-OUT.

SELLING BLESSINGS
The selling of good fortune, usually by preachers, using
candles and other objects which one receives and for which
one in turn leaves a donation. A blessing could be in the
form of a winning number buried within the candle or object that the person could play; the good fortune is received
when the number FALLS.

SEMI-BLACK
An African American who exploits the Black cause for his/
her own purpose, but who doesn't identify with the race;
Black only when it's convenient and serves one's own self-
interest.

SEND
To excite someone in a romantic/sexual sense. Resurfacing
of a term from the popular 1958 recording, "You Send
Me," by the late Sam Cooke.

SENT UP
Incarcerated; sentenced to time in prison. "All of them got
sent up."

SERIOUS

Superb, excellent; describes something or someone to be taken seriously because of profound quality, impressive accomplishment, or depth. "That is a serious car," that is, It is a beautiful, well-made car; "That was a serious cake," meaning, That is a very delicious, superb cake. Crossover term.

SERIOUS BIDNESS

See SQUARE BIDNESS.

SERVE

1) To provide sexual favors. "I just want to be the one to serve you." 2) To be outdone by a competitor. "He got served." 3) To beat up.

SET[1]

1) A gang or group. 2) Neighborhood. 3) A party or social gathering, usually small and intimate.

SET[2]

To defeat in the game of BID. "We got set."

SET BOOK

In BID, the cards played at the moment of victory; also used to refer to the card or cards in a player's hand that will be played to clinch the opposition's defeat. "Come wit it, I got yo set book right here."

SET IT OUT

See COME WIT IT.

SETTIN HAND

In BID, the cards in a player's hand that will constitute defeat for the opposition when played. As the SISTA said, "Yeah, Baby Sis, this settin hand is jes waitin for yo ass!"

SHADE TREE

See JACKLEG.

SHADES

Crossover term. See LOCS, newer term that has not crossed over.

SHAKE AND BAKE

1) In basketball, a set of moves where the offensive player with the ball tries to elude (*shake*) the player guarding or CHECKin him/her by executing a series of skillful movements, such as going from side to side on the court, faking, stop-and-go dribbling, etc. 2) By extension, any act of artful dodging.

SHEIK

A scarf worn by males over the hair and tied in back; suggests toughness/BADness.

SHERM

A type of mushroom used as a drug.

SHINE

A derogatory reference to a Black male; possibly derived from the glossy appearance of ebony skin. The hero of the folk toast (story) "Shine and the Sinking of the *Titanic*" is given this name. Though looked down upon by the white world, Shine ends up being the only survivor of the *Titanic* disaster of 1912. Because of his MOTHER WIT, he is the only one who realizes that this so-called technological marvel is about to go down, and he abandons ship.

THE SHIT

1) The height of something; the maximum. "This crib is the Shit," meaning, This is a fantastic house. 2) The chief person in charge. 3) The best, greatest, most accomplished person. "These men out here today [referring to single Black men] all think they the Shit," that is, The available men today are conceited and think they are the very best.

SHIT

1) Can refer to almost anything—possessions, events, etc. "He had on some bad shit," meaning, He was wearing stylish clothes; "We wasn't goin for they shit," that is, We refused to accept their abuse. See also CHICKEN SHIT, FULL OF SHIT, ON SOMEBODY'S SHIT LIST, PULL SHIT,

PUT SHIT ON SOMEBODY, SHOOT THE SHIT, SLICK
SHIT, TAKE SHIT, TALK SHIT, UP SHIT CREEK, WEAK
SHIT. 2) A filler with no meaning, just used to complete a
statement.

SHIT FROM SHINOLA
See ASS FROM A HOLE IN THE GROUND. "Oh, no, I ain
no fool by a long shot. I can tell shit from Shinola." "Shinola" is a brand name for an inexpensive and very strong-
smelling liquid shoe polish that once was widely used because it was cheap.

SHIT HIT THE FAN
A reference to the start of an incident, commotion, distur-
bance, argument, or conflict precipitated by some critical
statement, important action, or significant event. "Then my
momma said she didn't give a care who they was, and that's
when the shit hit the fan." Crossover expression.

SHIZ-OUT
See SHOUT OUT.

SHO YOU RIGHT
An expression of affirmation in response to what someone
has said or done. "Sure, you're right," pronounced according to AAE rules as *Sho you right;* see Introduction.

SHOOP
To have sex.

SHOOT DICE
To play craps, a gambling game.

SHOOT SOME HOOP
See B-BALL², HOOP².

SHOOT THE DIE
On urban B-BALL courts, where there are no referees, to
shoot from an agreed-upon line in order to determine various outcomes, as in deciding which team gets the ball at the
beginning of the game, resolving disagreements about fouls,
etc. For example, if a foul is called and the opposing player

disagrees, the player who called the foul shoots from this line, and if he makes the basket, then the alleged foul was an actual foul, but if he doesn't make it, then the alleged foul was not a foul. *Shooting the die* is viewed as impartial, unbiased. Derived from the older expression, SHOOTing DICE. See also LINE DON'T LIE.

SHOOT THE GIFT

See SHOOT THE SHIT. The *gift* here refers to the "gift of gab."

SHOOT THE SHIT

To engage in general conversational talk; to chit chat. Also *shoot the gift* (newer term); *talk shit* (older term); BUCK WHYLIN (older term, resurfacing).

SHORT

A car.

SHOT CALLER

One who calls the shots; the person running things; the authority.

SHOUT

1) To express religious/spiritual ecstasy, a state of deep emotion brought on by a religious experience; may be in the form of hollering, whooping, moaning. See also GIT HAPPY, GIT THE SPIRIT. 2) By extension, in the secular world, especially during performances at concerts, clubs, and in other places of entertainment, to express high emotion brought on by the musical entertainment, GITtin THE SPIRIT from the music.

SHOUT OUT

A greeting, a "hello," sent out to one's associates, friends, or supporters, often via the media. "Ima give a shout out to the posse over at Douglass High School" (from a call-in to a local radio DJ). Also sometimes *shiz-out*.

SHOW

The movies or a movie.

SHOW AND PROVE

1) To speak very articulately. 2) To provide hard, concrete proof of something.

SHOW SOME SIGN

A Traditional Black Church term referring to the importance of demonstrating one's religious fervor and the power and spirit of God by one's behavior, such as moaning or shouting.

SHOWBOAT

See GRANDSTAND.

SHUCKIN AND JIVIN

1) Putting someone on, deceiving a person. A useful strategy for accomplishing an objective when you are in a subordinate position without power. The enslaved African Frederick Douglass learned to read by *shuckin and jivin,* that is, by pretending that he already knew how to read and thereby tricking some white schoolboys into teaching him to read. 2) Saying that you are going to do something, but not really intending to do it.

SHUT THE NOISE!

A response of strong agreement or affirmation, meaning the opposite of what it says, that is, Keep on with the noise, Talk on, I'm WIT that! Also *Shut up!*

SHUT UP!

See SHUT THE NOISE!

SICK

Describes a person who is very funny, gets lots of laughs from telling jokes, humorous commentary, and acting CRAZY. Also *ill.*

SIG / SIG ON

See SIGNIFY / SIGNIFY ON.

SIGGIN

See SIGNIFYIN.

SIGNIFICATION

See SIGNIFYIN.

SIGNIFY/SIGNIFY ON

See SIGNIFYIN. Also *sig/sig on*.

SIGNIFYIN

The verbal art of ritualized insult, in which the speaker puts down, needles, talks about (*signifies on*) someone, to make a point or sometimes just for fun. It exploits the unexpected, using quick verbal surprises and humor, and it is generally characterized by nonmalicious and principled criticism. Also *siggin, signification*.

SILK

A reference to a white woman; derived from the stereotypical notion of the softness and silkiness of white hair.

SILLY

Foolish, lacking in good judgment.

SIMP

See LAME, SQUARE (older terms); GEEK (newer term).

SINGLE ACTION

A reference to PLAYing THE NUMBERS by betting on a single digit of the winning combination.

SINGLE ACTION LADY/MAN

See PICK-UP LADY/MAN.

By permission of the artist, Craig Rex Perry, and *Young Sisters and Brothers Ma*

SISSY

A derogatory term for a gay male.

SISTA

Any African American woman. Derived from the Traditional Black Church pattern of referring to female members of the Church "family" as *Sista*.

SISTA REA

Singing DIVA Aretha Franklin.

SKEEZE

To engage in a sexual orgy; done by RAP groupies.

SKEEZER

A person who has sex indiscriminately, especially a groupie. Also *scank* (older term).

SKIN

See GIVE SOMEBODY SKIN / SOME SKIN.

...ission of the artist, Craig Rex Perry, and *Young Sisters and Brothers Magazine*.

SKINNIN AND GRINNIN

Refers to a person who is happy and showing it, GIVing FIVE (*skinnin*) and smiling from ear to ear (*grinnin*) because everything's all right in his/her world.

SKINS

1) Females. 2) Euphemism for PUSSY. See also GIT SKINS, IN THE SKINS. 3) Cigarette papers for rolling marijuana cigarettes. 4) Fried pork rinds. 5) Drums; the term dates from the 1930s but is still in use by musicians today. 6) Shoes made from animal skins, such as alligator and lizard.

SKUNK

A low-down, no-good person; someone who is treacherous, LOW-LIFE.

SKY

See HOPS (newer term).

SLACK

See CUT SOMEBODY SOME SLACK.

SLAM

To have sex. See also SLAMMIN PARTNER.

SLAM-DUNK

1) To dump the basketball into the basket from over the rim with aggressive power and force, usually using both hands; harder and more powerful than a DUNK. 2) By extension, to make any aggressive, powerful move. A Black debater referring to a recent debate competition between university forensics teams: "Yeah, I beat em; just slam-dunked they asses."

SLAMMIN

1) Dumping or DUNKin the basketball in a strong, powerful, aggressive way; short for SLAM-DUNKin. 2) See DEF.

SLAMMIN PARTNER

One's sex partner; a partner in a relationship for sex only.

SLANG[1]
>   Young people's talk.

SLANG[2]
>   To sell crack and cocaine.

SLAVE
>   See HAIM.

SLEEF
>   See FIFTY-ONE.

SLICK
>   Clever; describes a person capable of manipulating people and situations to his/her advantage. Often grudgingly admired for this ability; however, see NICKEL SLICK.

SLICK SHIT
>   A clever move designed to get what you want.

SLIDE
>   1) To let a person off the hook; to excuse somebody. 2) To leave.

SLING
>   See SLANG[2].

SLIPPIN AND SLIDIN
>   1) Sneaking around; doing something under cover. 2) Sly behavior or camouflaged talk designed to mask one's real intentions or motives.

SLOB
>   An insulting name used by the Los Angeles gang, the CRIPS, for their former rivals, the BLOODS. Also *blob*.

SLOPE
>   To take a person down; to DIS someone.

SLOW JAM
>   A slow dance song.

SLOW YOUR/MY/HIS/HER/ etc., ROLL
>   To reduce the momentum of something.

SMACK¹

1) Low-grade cocaine, adulterated with fillers. 2) Heroin (older usage). 3) Drugs in general.

SMACK²

To talk negatively about somebody; to talk MESS about somebody.

SMOKE¹

Marijuana.

SMOKE²

1) To outdo someone in a competition. 2) To beat someone up. 3) To kill someone. 4) To ingest crack cocaine.

SMOKER

See CRACKHEAD. Also *puffer, rock star.*

SMOKIN

1) Performing excellently; doing something superbly. "The Rappers was smokin at the concert." 2) Smoking crack, commonly done in a small pipe. "My man done start smokin again," meaning, The speaker's friend has gone back to using crack after having been in drug therapy and off crack for several months.

SMOOTH

Dressed stylishly; looking good.

SNAKE

1) A sneaky person. 2) An informant; a snitch.

SNAPPER

A male's term for superb sex from a woman, specifically referring to intense, vigorous vaginal muscle movements during lovemaking. See also BITE.

SNORT

To ingest cocaine, or sometimes heroin, by sniffing it into the nostrils. Crossover term.

SNOW

A white person.

SNOW BUNNY
> A white female.

SOLID
> A response of affirmation or agreement. Crossover term.

SOME
> Sex; used by males or females. "I was wondering when he was gon give me some." See also NONE.

SOMEBODY
> See BE SOMEBODY.

SOONER
> 1) A person or thing that is cheap, shabby, not prime. 2) A mongrel dog, not a purebred; a dog that would "soon as be one thing as another."

SORRY
> Useless, ineffective, inadequate. "That lil party was the sorriest thing I ever been to."

SOUL
> The essence of life; feeling, passion, emotional depth—all of which are believed to be derived from struggle, suffering, and having participated in the Black Experience. Having risen above the suffering, the person gains *soul*.

SOUL BROTHA/ SISTA
> A generic reference to an African American man/woman, a member of the community of SOULful folk.

SOUL CLAP
> A three-beat rhythmic unit of overlapping claps, with one regular clap on the beat rapidly followed by two quick claps off the beat.

SOUL FOOD
> Cuisine characteristic of African Americans, such as red beans and rice, CHITLINS, greens, crackling bread, black-eyed peas, etc.

SOUL SHAKE

An intricate handshake to demonstrate solidarity; very popular during the 1960s and 1970s. Also known as the "Black Power handshake." Probably from the Traditional Black Church concept and practice of extending the RIGHT HAND OF FELLOWSHIP. The *soul shake* has a number of complex variations on the basic structure, which is executed by juxtaposing the right thumbs, placing your thumb first to the right of the other person's thumb, then to the left, next, grasping the other person's fingers in your palm, followed by your fingers being grasped in his palm.

SOUL SOUND

Music that is s o u Lful and rooted in Blackness and the African American Experience; the term is applied particularly

Living in the suburbs has its disadvantages.

to rhythm and blues and the music of the 1960s and 1970s.
An older expression, resurfacing along with OLD SCHOOL
music in HIP HOP. "The . . . R & B, hip hop soul sound of
songstress Mary J. Blige [who has] redefined R & B . . . by
bringing in elements of hip hop and soul. . . . Mary's unique
blend of old school groove, hip hop and jazzy vocals have
shot *What's the* 4 1 1? straight to the top" (from "Real
Love: The Mary J. Blige Story," in *Word Up!*).

SPADE
A reference to any African American; a derogatory term.

SPIRIT
See GIT THE SPIRIT.

SPLEEFER
See FIFTY-ONE.

SPLIB
A generic reference to any Black person; a fairly neutral
term.

SPONSOR
A man who supports, or contributes significantly to the
support of, a woman in exchange for sexual favors; a man
with a "kept woman."

SPOOK
A derogatory reference to an African American.

SPORT
1) To dress stylishly and attractively. 2) To spend money on
someone; usually said about a man of means spending
money on a woman (older usage). Not to be confused with
TRICKIN, which involves a man spending money on a
woman that he ain got no business spending.

SPRINGS
See HOPS.

SPRUNG
Hopelessly in love; out of emotional control.

SQUARE

1) A person who is uninformed, lacking in sophistication, unHIP. This meaning has crossed over. Also *lame, geek, simp*. 2) A cigarette. This meaning has not crossed over.

SQUARE BIDNESS

A phrase tacked onto a statement to indicate that a statement or action has integrity, is serious, appropriate, sincere, on the up-and-up. "My boy gon do the work, square bidness." Derived from the Masonic tradition, in which the compass and the square are essential tools for a Mason. An upright man is a "square" man, who acts and deals with integrity, which is what the Masonic tradition teaches. Also *serious bidness*.

SQUASH

1) To argue. 2) To fight.

SQUASH IT

1) Resolve the matter once and for all. 2) Forget it, disregard it.

STACY ADAMS

A popular, high-fashion brand of shoes for men; used for STYLIN AND PROFILIN.

STALLION

See FOX.

STAR

See FOX.

STATIC

Confusion, trouble, conflict; something you don't want to hear.

STAY IN THE STREET

To be away from home a lot, always on the go. See also IN THE STREET.

STEADY

Indicates something done frequently and continuously.

"Them fools be steady hustlin everybody they see."

STEP[1]

> A fraternity or sorority marching move, with intricate patterns, or steps; portrayed in Spike Lee's film *School Daze*. See also STEP SHOW.

STEP[2]

> 1) To leave. 2) To perform fraternity or sorority marching moves.

STEP OFF

> GIT OUT MY FACE; leave me alone.

STEP SHOW

> Intricate marching steps and movements performed by fraternities and sororities. See also STEP[1].

STEP TO

> To challenge someone to a fight.

STEPPIN

> 1) Walking, often with a decisive purpose; applies to males or females. From Sonia Sanchez's poem "Queens of the Universe": "Black women/the only Queens of the Universe/though we be stepping unqueenly sometime." 2) Walking on indoor skates, not gliding in the usual way, but walking in slower, albeit intricate, steps.

STICK IT

> Refers to what the male does during sex.

STIFF

> A person who is stuffy, no fun.

STOCKING CAP

> A head covering made by cutting off the lower part of a woman's nylon stocking; fits tight and keeps the hair in place.

STOMP

> To beat up; to hurt someone badly.

STONE

> Added before a word for emphasis, as in *stone fine,* meaning very beautiful; *stone tired,* meaning extremely tired. See also COAL (newer intensifying term).

STONE TO THE BONE

> Describes a person who has all positive qualities in great abundance.

STOOPID

> Also *stupid.* See DEF.

STORY

> An explanation, usually elaborate and extended, to account for something or justify one's behavior; generally fictionalized and exaggerated, but could also be a *story* with a kernel of truth that gets blown up in the telling.

STRAIGHT

> 1) OKAY; all right; good. 2) Describes a person who has drugs for sale (older usage). "If you lookin, Bo's straight."

STRAIGHT UP

> Directly, straightforwardly, honestly, frankly; stating the honest unmitigated truth; boldly expressing one's thinking and/or feelings. Crossover expression.

STRAIGHTEN

> To treat hair with a chemical RELAXER or to use a HOT COMB on it to remove the natural tight (KINKY) curls.

STRAIGHTEN UP AND FLY RIGHT

> 1) Get serious, stop playing around. Older meaning. This use has crossed over. 2) Come out of the streets, stop running around, and settle down.

STRAP

> Carrying a gun. "Strapped" pronounced according to AAE rules; see Introduction.

STRAPPED

> See STRAP.

STRAWBERRY

See HEAD HUNTER. For the male version, see RASP-BERRY.

STRAY PIECE

A sexual encounter, usually a one-time event, with a female other than a male's wife or steady WOMAN. See also PIECE.

STRENGTH

See ON THE STRENGTH.

STRIDES

Shoes.

STRIDIN

Soulful, rhythmic walking.

STROKE

The act of sex performed by the male.

STRONG

Indicates a particularly bold or noteworthy assertion, one that shows mental toughness. "That's some strong stuff you talkin!" Related to, and probably the source of, the newer expression, ON THE STRENGTH.

STRONGER THAN RED DEVIL LYE

Superstrong. Red Devil is the brand of lye that was used in CONKin men's hair during Malcolm X's era.

STRUNG OUT

1) Addicted to drugs. Crossover meaning. 2) By extension, obsessed with or hung up on any person or activity. "My man is strung out behind this new lady he just copped."

STRUT

Soulful, rhythmic walking, especially done when one is G'D UP and SHOWBOATin.

STRUT YOUR STUFF

To display your wares, knowledge, dress, or whatever; show 'em what you got. Crossover expression.

STUFF¹

1) Euphemism for PUSSY. 2) Anything extraordinary. 3) Crack.

STUFF²

To DUNK the basketball, to stuff it in the basket.

STUPID

Also *stoopid*. See DEF.

STYLIN AND PROFILIN

Adopting a cool, poised, confident posture, and usually dressed stylishly/FLY; appearing CHILLed and in control.

SUGAR

1) A form of address for females; used by males, but a neutral term, does not convey romance or intimacy. 2) Homosexuality. See also SWEET.

SUP?

See WHASSUP?

SUPERFLY

Exceptionally upscale; ultra exciting and with-it. From the 1970s film by that name.

SUPERMARKET CONVERSATION

Empty, meaningless chatter, i.e., like the music played in supermarkets.

SURE, YOU'RE RIGHT

See SHO YOU RIGHT.

SWEAT

1) To bother or hassle someone. 2) To proposition someone.

SWEET

1) Outstanding; very nice. 2) Refers to a gay male; not as derogatory as PUNK or *faggot*, but still bordering on the negative.

SWEET-TALK

A style of talk using words of endearment and promises for

the purpose of persuading someone to do or think what you want them to; often a CONVERSATION or a RAP in male-female relationships.

SWEETIE

A form of address used by males to address any female; does not necessarily convey intimacy.

SWEP

Refers to the state of being strongly in love, vulnerable due to one's affections for another. From "swept," i.e., swept away by one's emotions, rendered in AAE pronunciation as *swep;* see Introduction. Also NOSE OPEN, GOT HIS/HER NOSE, GOT HIS/HER NOSE OPEN.

SWEPT

See SWEP.

SWOOP

To take someone else's man or woman in a short amount of time.

SYSTEM

The criminal justice system—not only jail, but bail, parole, awaiting sentencing, probation, undergoing trial, etc. "Ain heard from Joe in a while. Hope he ain in the system." In the previous generation, *system* referred to the dominant society and the Eurocentric political and economic realm of the United States. The resurfacing and narrowed meaning of the term reflects the deteriorating condition of African Americans since 1980, resulting in an astronomical increase in the number of African American males in various levels of the criminal justice system. In the age group 20–29, there are more Black men involved in the *system* than are enrolled in college. And in the age group 15–19, in some urban districts there are more Black men involved in the *system* than are graduating from high school.

T

A T

A precise and exact match or fit. "These shoes match yo hat to a T"; "That dress fit you to a T."

TABLE PIMPS

See CRUMB SNATCHERS.

TAKE A CHILL PILL

See CHILL.

TAKE A TEXT

1) In a Traditional Black Church service, to announce the Scriptural reference and message of a sermon, a fairly elaborate ritual with a set formula involving the reading of the Scriptural passage and a reinterpretation using a contemporary, cleverly worded theme. 2) By extension, to *take a text* on a person is to tell that person off in an elaborate, dramatic manner, using SIGNIFYIN and other forms from the Verbal Tradition. See also READ.

TAKE CARE OF BIDNESS

To seriously attend to or complete something; to get on with something, get down to business. Also *TCB*.

TAKE IT TO THE HOOP

1) In B-BALL, to move the ball all the way to the basket and make the shot. 2) By extension, to go all the way with something; to go down to the wire and succeed; to perform something superbly.

TAKE LOW

To assume a posture of humility in order to defuse conflict and achieve an objective. "Take low and go," that is, Humble yourself, and you'll succeed in whatever you're trying to accomplish.

TAKE OUT

1) To outdo a competitor. 2) To kill. Crossover meaning.

TAKE SHIT
To accept abuse or mistreatment from someone. Crossover expression.

TAKING NO SHORTS
Not to be taken advantage of.

TALK SHIT
1) To talk nonsense, nothingness; to bullshit. This meaning has crossed over. 2) See SHOOT THE SHIT. See also BUCK WHYLIN.

TALK THAT TALK
To use the forms of the African American Verbal Tradition in an intense, creative, dynamic, energetic style; an expression indicating the speaker is RAPpin in a powerful, convincing manner.

TALKIN HEAD
Someone who is arguing and wants to fight.

TALKIN IN TONGUE
In the Traditional Black Church, speaking in a secret, coded language while SHOUTin and undergoing spirit-possession.

TALKIN OUT THE SIDE OF YOUR NECK / MOUTH
Lying, deceiving; TALKin SHIT.

TALKIN SMACK
Talking junk, nonsense; bullshitting.

TALKIN TRASH
1) The art of DISsin one's opponent during competitive play (as in basketball, Nintendo, BID) so as to erode their confidence, get them rattled or distracted so they'll make poor plays and lose the game. 2) The art of using strong, rhythmic, clever talk and forms in the African American Verbal Tradition—e.g., SIGNIFYIN, WOOFin—to entertain, to promote one's ego, to establish leadership in a group, or to project an image of BADness.

TALL PAPER
See BIG PAPER.

TASTE
> Liquor or wine.

TCB
> Take care of business. See TAKE CARE OF BIDNESS.

TEAR THE ROOF OFF THE SUCKA!
> To PAR-TAY; to have BIG FUN.

TELEPHONE NUMBER
> A long prison sentence.

TELL IT!
> See TELL THE TRUTH!

TELL THE TRUTH!
> An enthusiastic response affirming what someone has said or done. Also *Tell it!*

TENDER
> A young, desirable female or male. Also *tenderoni.*

TENDERONI
> See TENDER.

TERRIBLE
> See DEF (newer term).

TESTIFY
> 1) In the Traditional Black Church, to give affirmation to the power and truth of something; when GITtin THE SPIRIT, people often *testify.* 2) By extension, to celebrate through verbal acknowledgment the greatness of anything, or one's strong feelings about something.

TG
> In gang terminology, a young member; literally, Tiny Gangster.

THAT HOW YOU LIVIN?
> Why are you acting like that?

THAT YOU?
> Is the item, person, song, whatever, yours or your type of thing?

THAT'S ALL SHE WROTE
> An expression used to refer to the end of something; can be something that leaves either good or bad memories. After eating a huge, delectable serving of CHITLINS, Ralph said, "Well, that's all she wrote!"

THAT'S MIGHTY WHITE OF YOU!
> A SIGNIFYIN expression referring to someone patronizing you or making up your mind for you; from the perception that whites typically do this to Blacks.

THERE IT IS
> A response meaning "That's how it is," "That's the way it goes"; conveys a sense of surrendering to the finality and inevitability of an event or situation. The expression dates from the 1960s; now resurfacing and expanding meaning in HIP HOP, as in the 1993 money-making hit JAMS by two different RAP groups, Tag Team's "Whoomp! (There It Is)" and 95 South's "Whoot, There It Is."

THICK
> 1) See DIESEL (newer term). 2) Describes a large penis. 3) Being intimate, close friends with someone.

THICK LIPS
> See BIG LIPS.

THIRD STRUGGLE
> The struggle against sexual weaknesses and unprincipled sexual affairs, in the vocabulary of activists.

THOUGHT LIKE LIT
> A response to a person trying to explain away or excuse an error. From the first line of the familiar little rhyme from the Oral Tradition:

> You thought like lit
> Thought you farted,
> but you shit.

THREADS

1) Stylish clothes or outfit. 2) Clothes in general. Crossover meaning.

THREE-SIX-NINE (3-6-9)

Euphemism for *shit*. The SISTA said, "You know men, they always comin up with some 3-6-9, jes when you least expect it." From the numerological sign for the *shit role* in DREAM BOOKS. Used for its symbolic significance in Ralph Ellison's novel *Invisible Man*, where the home of the main character became an underground sewer with 1,369 light bulbs.

THREE-SIXTY-FIVE (3-65)

Refers to something done on a continuous basis; literally, 365 days a year.

THROUGH

1) Exasperated, annoyed with someone or something. 2) Emotionally exhausted, outdone, completely taken aback by an action or statement. See also ALL THE WAY THROUGH.

THROW / THROW DOWN

1) To do something vigorously, to the limit. To *throw down* at a party is to have an exceptionally good time, BIG FUN. *Throwin down* in school is excelling at your studies. 2) To have sex. 3) To fight.

THROW A BRICK

To commit a crime; do something wrong or illegal. "Money been so hard to come by I'm thinkin about throwin a brick."

THROW BONES

1) To play dominoes. 2) To shoot dice.

THROW THE D / THROW THE P

To have sex.

THROW THE GIFT

To talk to a person romantically in order to captivate that

person's heart. The *gift* refers to the "gift of gab." See also
HIT ON.

THROW UP A BRICK

In basketball, to miss the basket and hit the backboard or
rim with an ugly sound. Not to be confused with THROW A
BRICK.

THUMP

To fight.

TIGHT

1) Describes people who are intimates, close friends or associates. 2) Describes a person's business/GAME as well-or-
ganized, in place, the way it's supposed to be. "Now, the
Brotha's game is tight, all right."

TIGHT AS DICK'S HATBAND

Extremely stingy. Also *tight as Jimmy's hatband* (newer version).

TIGHT AS JIMMY'S HATBAND

See TIGHT AS DICK'S HATBAND.

TI-IS

To tell it like it is; speak the truth in a frank, forthright
manner.

TIME

A reference to the political or psychological state or mood
of things. *What time it is* refers to the real deal, the truth,
the real story, what's actually occurring at the moment; not
a fantasy. If you know *what time it is,* you're UP ON IT,
HIP, knowledgeable, a survivor.

TIP[1]

1) A person's GAME, one's own Thang, some aspect of you
that makes you *you.* Legendary singer James Brown, in his
"I'm Real" JAM, chides all the HIP HOP Rappers who are
sampling freely from his old hits, telling them to get off his
tip. 2) Used in combination with another word, *tip* refers to
the essence of that particular word. *On a bullshit tip* means

"bullshit." *On the gangsta tip* means "GANGSTA."

TIP²

To have an affair outside one's monogamous relationship.

TIRED

Stale, old hat; inappropriate, PLAYED OUT. "Yo shit is tired." A popular term among women.

TITTIES

See BUMPIN TITTIES.

TLC

Tender, loving care. Crossover term.

TOE UP

Drunk. The body is "torn up," rendered in AAE as *toe up;* see Introduction.

TOGETHA

1) Describes any place, event, idea, or thing that is great, effective, in order. 2) Describes an accomplished individual, someone who has *got it togetha* (see GIT IT TOGETHA), which has crossed over although *togetha* has not.

TOKEN

An African American placed in a job or social position, usually due to pressure or demands from Blacks. However, the person does nothing to promote the Black cause and, in fact, has been put in the position only to showcase a Black presence and quiet African American protest. The term came into widespread usage in the COMMUNITY during the Black Freedom Struggle of the 1960s and 1970s, wherein a few African Americans were moved into the economic mainstream as a result of marches, sit-ins, and other forms of Black activism and REBELLION.

TOM

A negative reference to a Black person, suggesting that he/she is a SELL-OUT, not DOWN WITH the Black cause. *Tom* comes from the character Uncle Tom in Harriet Beecher

Stowe's *Uncle Tom's Cabin,* who put his master's wishes and life before his own. *Dr. Thomas* SIGNIFIES ON an educated *Tom.* The terms *Aunt* and *Uncle* recall the Southern custom of whites addressing *all* Blacks as "aunt" or "aunty" and "uncle," a practice resented by Blacks. Also *Uncle Tom, Uncle Thomas;* for women, *Aunt Thomasina, Aunt Jane.*

TOO THROUGH

See ALL THE WAY THROUGH.

TORN UP

See TOE UP.

TOTALED

1) Ugly. 2) All messed up.

TREY EIGHT

A .38-caliber gun.

TRICK

1) A person who can be easily manipulated. 2) A customer of a prostitute. Crossover meaning.

TRICKERATION

The act of PLAYing on, deceiving someone; manipulation to lead someone astray.

TRICKIN

Having sex for money.

TRICKNOLOGY

European American technological innovations, viewed as things to be distrusted, as often being not technology, but *tricknology.* Popularized by The NATION.

TRIFLIN

Describes a person who fails to do something that he/she is capable of doing; inadequate, lazy, having no get-up-and-go.

TRIM

Sex from a woman; euphemism for PUSSY.

TRIP SOMEONE OUT

1) To cause an unusual, pleasurable reaction in someone, by actions or by statements. 2) To cause a surprise reaction in someone.

TRIPPIN

1) Fantasizing about something, acting irrationally. Also *illin* (newer term). 2) Doing something outside the norm, above the usual in a positive way.

TRUCKIN

1) Running fast. See also JET (newer term); MOTOR, FLY (older terms). 2) Going somewhere; moving forward with a purpose. 3) Strolling.

TRUTH BE TOLD

An expression of validity; usually occurs at the beginning of a statement, emphasizing the truth of the statement. "Truth be told, boyfriend done run out of DUCKETTES," meaning, It may not be widely known, but the fact of the matter is that this man has run out of money.

TUDE

1) An aggressive, arrogant, defiant, I-know-I'm-BAD pose or air about oneself. 2) An oppositional, negative outlook or disposition. Also *attitude*.

TURF

1) Your street or HOOD. Crossover meaning. 2) By extension, any endeavor or topic of conversation that you know well and lay claim to. "They up there tryin to talk about math and numbers, that's yo girl's turf."

TURKISH

Heavy, elaborate, flashy gold jewelry.

TURN A BOOK

In BID, to win a round of play.

TURN SOMEBODY OUT

To introduce a person to something alien to them, generally

something not in their best interests.

TURN SOMETHING OUT

1) To create a scene, causing people to vacate a place. 2) To party aggressively, loudly, and with wild abandon, partying until the place is emptied out.

TWENTY CENTS

1) Twenty dollars. 2) A quantity (BAG) of marijuana selling for twenty dollars. Also *twinkie*.

TWENTY-FOE-SEVEN (24-7)

Twenty-four hours a day, seven days a week; used to describe something that is continuous, that appears to be happening nonstop. "The only way we got ovah was that my daddy work twenty-foe-seven."

TWINKIE

1) A twenty-dollar bill. 2) A quantity (BAG) of marijuana selling for twenty dollars. Also *twenty cents*.

TWISTED

Acting irrationally; not behaving like one's usual self; mixed-up.

TWO-MINUTE BROTHA

A man who performs sex only for a very short time, in the talk of women.

V

UAW

You ain working; also, You ain white. Created by African American workers to put the United Automobile Workers, or UAW, on FRONT STREET for its racism and failure to protect the jobs of Black workers.

UNCLE THOMAS
1) Associate justice of the Supreme Court Clarence Thomas. 2) See TOM.

UNCLE TOM
See TOM.

UNDERGROUND HIT
1) A record that is a hit in the COMMUNITY and out in the street, but doesn't make it to the mainstream. 2) A record not made in a studio, not professionally recorded.

UP ON IT
Well-informed, highly aware of something; sophisticated; HIP.

UP SHIT CREEK
In serious trouble; vulnerable to exposure or defeat; in danger of losing something. Crossover expression.

UP SOUTH
The North; coined by Malcolm X. See DOWN SOUTH.

UPSIDE THE HEAD
See GO UPSIDE SOMEBODY'S HEAD.

UPTIGHT
Full of anxiety; stressed out about something. Crossover term.

USG
United States Ghetto. A SIGNIFYIN characterization speaking to the racism of the system that has created "inner cities," concentrations of African Americans of the working, and increasingly UN-working, class in every major U.S. city. Fredro Starr of the RAP group Onyx: "We're from New York but we're in LA and it's still the ghetto. You go to Washington, it's ghetto, everywhere it's ghetto. . . . We don't represent the USA, we represent the USG. . . . You got the USA and we got the USG. We ain't really from the USA because we really ain't got no props in the USA, so we relate our shit to the USG" (from *The Source*, June 1993).

VAPORS

1) An opportunistic desire for someone who was previously shunned, but who now has status or material possessions. "It wasn't until I got that recording contract that she caught the vapors." 2) Jealousy. 3) Crack smoke.

VEE-IN

An initiation ritual used by gangs.

VERDICT

1) Something that's going to happen; the plan. 2) The final word about a subject; the outcome. "So what is the verdict? Are we goin to the show tonight or what?"

VIBE[1]

1) Used in reference to the way one KICKS IT or HANGS, that is, the way a person carries him/herself, their RAP, their style, especially when relating to the opposite sex. "I wanna see you . . . wanna meet you and see how you vibe." 2) To date or maintain a relationship with someone. "The Brotha and I been vibin for a couple of months now."

VIBE[2]

1) Intuition; a hunch. 2) The elusive, indefinable quality of something that can't be described, you have to feel it. This use of *vibe* has crossed over in the form "vibes."

VICIOUS

See DEF.

VINE / VINES

A male's suit. Probably from the idea that when it really fits, it hangs as do vines in nature.

VOODOO

A religion with roots in West Africa; the belief system is polytheistic (many gods) and includes demons and the "living dead"; practices include the use of rituals, charms, herbs, and potions to control reality and events. The word *Voodoo,* meaning "protective spirit," comes from Dahomey (now Benin) in West Africa and is derived from *Vodu* in the Fon and Ewe languages. Members of this religious sect reside throughout the United States, but the largest concentration of members is still in New Orleans, the birthplace of *Voodoo* in North America. African American writer and anthropologist Zora Neale Hurston was initiated into the religion in New Orleans in the 1920s and presents detailed accounts in her writings.

Although *Voodoo* relies on a system of magic, as is true of all religions, this is not its fundamental aspect. In Africa it was used to unite groups to fight against a common enemy, and during enslavement in North America, it became a force to organize, rally, and strengthen those rebelling against enslavement. This was probably the primary reason for slavemasters' attempts to suppress *Voodoo* as a religion by banning religious meetings and services. With the outlawing of the religious aspect, the magic aspect—the use of charms and herbal rituals, the creation of *Voodoo* objects, etc.—became more pronounced, since Ole Massa viewed the magic as only so much primitive "hocus-pocus." In 1945 the World Order of Congregational Churches gave its official stamp of approval to *Voodoo* as a legitimate religion. However, the association of the religion with "primitive" magic, and especially the HOODOO MAN's manipulation and exploitation of the magic element for profit, widespread in the Black community by the 1940s, drove genuine *Voodoo* followers underground. Although *Voodoo* is not widely practiced in the U.S. Black community today, it is fairly prevalent in Haiti, other parts of the Caribbean, and Brazil. What does still exist in the community today is a belief that Blacks have supernatural powers, a belief that comes out of the tradition and religious system of *Voodoo* in the community. See also HOODOO.

W

WACK

Not with-it; undesirable; not good.

WANNABE

1) An African American trying to be white, acting white; in Spike Lee's *School Daze,* the *wannabes* opposed the Black-oriented "jigaboos." 2) By extension, a person trying to act as if he/she is a member of any group or has achieved a particular status that he/she does not have. 3) Someone trying to be a gang member.

WASTE

1) To kill. 2) To spill something. 3) See also GIT WASTED.

WATCH MEETING NIGHT

New Year's Eve, when Traditional Black Church folk gather to "watch" the old year go out and welcome the new one in, giving thanks to God that they have made it through the year.

WAVE NOUVEAU

A chemically STRAIGHTENed hairstyle; gets curly when wet, but a controlled curl that doesn't NAP UP.

WAX¹

A record album or label. "To be put on *wax*" means to sign a recording contract.

WAX²

1) To defeat someone in competition. "We waxed dem nig-gaz by 40 points" (referring to defeating the opposing team in B-BALL). 2) To energetically and strongly do something to the maximum.

WAX SOME ASS
To have sex.

WEAK SHIT
1) Insufficient or inadequate action, words, or behavior. "Don't come in here with no weak shit, cause I ain goin for it," i.e., Please don't bother me with an insubstantial explanation because I won't accept it. 2) In sports competition, a subpar performance.

WEAK SIDE
1) A point of vulnerability in sports competition or in one's argument or ideas about something. 2) Refers to something that is in poor condition or cheap.

WEAR FACE
To use or apply facial makeup.

WEAR OUT ONE'S WELCOME
Used by senior Blacks to indicate that: 1) A person has exhausted his or her acceptability in a group or situation. 2) A person has exceeded the limits of hospitality.

WEAR YOU / THEM / IT / etc., OUT
1) To have sex. 2) To outdo somebody in a competitive situation, such as cards or sports.

WEAVE
A female hairdo with synthetic or human hair braided into the natural hair at the roots, with the rest left loose for a long, full-looking hairstyle.

WEED
Marijuana.

WEIGHT
1) Blame. 2) Psychological or emotional pressure.

WELL, ALL RIGHT!
A response of affirmation or enthusiastic endorsement.

WHAM BAM, THANK YOU, MAM!
An older expression resurfacing in HIP HOP, as in the

RAP JAM "What's the 4 1 1?" by DIVA Mary J. Blige: "I don't have no time for no 'Wham bam, thank you, Mam!'/ Gas me up, git me drunk, and hit the skins and scram." See BIP BAM, THANK YOU, MAM!

WHASS HAPNIN?

A greeting pattern, "What's happening?" meaning, Hello, how are you? WHASSUP? and WHAT UP?, newer terms, are variations on this older pattern.

WHASSUP?

1) "What's up?" Also *Sup?*, *What up?* See also WHASS HAPNIN? 2) In Los Angeles gang usage, a generic password.

WHASSUP WITH THAT?

"What is up with that?," an expression requesting clarity or information on something, literally, "What is the status of X?"

WHAT GO ROUND COME ROUND

A proverb that expresses perhaps the essence of traditional "root culture" Blacks' beliefs about life, that whatever has happened before will occur again, even if in a different form. In a study of over a thousand proverbs used by African Americans, this was found to be the most frequently used proverb in the African American community (study conducted by Jack L. Daniel, Geneva Smitherman-Donaldson, and Milford Jeremiah, reported in "'Makin A Way Outa No Way': The Proverb Tradition in the Black Experience," *Journal of Black Studies,* June 1987).

WHAT IT B LIKE?

1) A greeting among members of the L.A. gang the BLOODS. See also WHAT IT C LIKE? 2) A general greeting among non–gang members (older usage).

WHAT IT C LIKE?

A greeting among members of the L.A. gang the CRIPS.

WHAT TIME IT IS
See TIME.

WHAT UP?
As a greeting pattern, becoming more frequent as WHAS-SUP? crosses over. "What's up" becomes *What up* as a result of an AAE pronunciation rule. See Introduction.

WHAT'S HAPPENING?
See WHASS HAPNIN?

WHAT'S UP?
See WHASSUP?, WHAT UP?

WHAT'S UP WITH THAT?
See WHASSUP WITH THAT?

WHIS
See BID.

WHISSIN
Playing BID.

WHIST
See WHIS.

WHITE WHITE
1) A EUROPEAN AMERICAN who acts extremely "white," in a cultural sense; one completely lacking in knowledge of the Black sensibility and devoid of COOLNESS. 2) A very racist European American.

WHITEMAIL
Activists' and AFRICAN-CENTERED folks' emerging term for "blackmail." Reflects an effort to reverse negative images of Blackness in the English language.

WHITENIZATION
A reference to the early historical process of Europeanizing the United States through promotion of Euro-American values, culture, politics, ideology, patterns of thinking, and social habits.

WHITEY
A derisive term for a white person. Also *honky*.

WHOLE LOTTA YELLUH WASTED
Used in reference to an unattractive light-complexioned African American; usually a person who has light skin but African facial features and hair. The YELLUH is "wasted" in the sense that this myth is based on light skin as a valuable commodity, but since the *yelluh* is ugly, the light skin is doing that person no good.

THE WHOLE NINE
Everything; all of something. AAE version of the general slang phrase, "the whole nine yards."

WHORE
See HO.

WIGGA
A WIGGER, literally, a white NIGGER, an emerging positive term for white youth who identify with HIP HOP, RAP, and other aspects of African American Culture. Throughout U.S. history, there have always been *wiggas*, and particularly in the twentieth century. In the 1950s, white writer Norman Mailer dubbed them "white Negroes." Their numbers are significantly larger today than in previous generations because of the exposure to African American Culture made possible by television. See also NIGGA.

WIGGER
See WIGGA.

WILD
See RUN WILD.

WILDERNESS
The North American continent, especially the United States.

WINDY CITY
Chicago. Crossover expression. Also *Chi-town,* which has not crossed over.

WIT

> Indicates approval of something; in favor of a thing, person, idea, or action. "I ain't wit being broke; I'm wit money." AAE rendering of "with"; see Introduction.

WIT THE PROGRAM

> Agreeable to a plan of action, activity, idea, or event.

WITH

> See WIT.

WITH THE PROGRAM

> See WIT THE PROGRAM.

WITNESS

> See BEAR WITNESS.

WOLF

> See WOOF.

WOMAN

> A man's girlfriend or wife; used by men and women. See also LADY.

WHERE I'M COMING FROM   BY BARBARA BRANDON

WHERE I'M COMING FROM copyright 1992 Barbara Brandon. Dist. by UNIVERSAL PRESS SYNDI
Reprinted with permission. All rights re

WOMANISH

See WOMNISH.

WOMANIST

An African American feminist; also used to refer to Black feminist thought. The term was popularized by Alice Walker, author of *The Color Purple* (which won a Pulitzer Prize and was made into a film by Steven Spielberg). A *womanist* is rooted in the COMMUNITY and committed to the survival and development of herself and the community at the same time. In keeping with her emphasis on the importance of using language that is "organic" to the African American community, Walker appropriated the term from the AAE word WOMANISH. She writes: "*Womanist* . . . From the black folk expression of mothers to female children, 'You acting womanish,' i.e., like a woman . . . Wanting to know more and in greater depth than is considered 'good' for one . . . Acting grown up . . . Interchangeable with another black folk expression: 'You trying to be grown.' Responsible. In charge. *Serious*" (from *In Search of our Mothers' Gardens,* published by Harcourt Brace Jovanovich, 1983).

WOMLISH

See WOMNISH.

WOMNISH

Also rendered in AAE as *womlish.* Acting like a grown, adult woman; often used to reprimand young girls who are acting too grown-up for their age. Also *womanish.* See also MANNISH.

WOOD

1) A white person; see PECKAWOOD. 2) A Cadillac car, Fleetwood model, once a popular symbol of LIVIN LARGE.

WOOF

To threaten by using boastful, strong language; the *woofer* may or may not intend to execute the threat. One who believes the *woofin* may challenge the *woofer,* in which case the person is said to have *bought the woof ticket.* Probably from the AAE pronunciation of "wolf"; see Introduction.

WOOF TICKET

A verbal threat, which one *sells* to somebody; may or may not be real. Often used as a strategy to make another person back down and surrender to what that person perceives as a superior power.

WOOFER

See WOOF.

WORD! / WORD UP!

A response of affirmation. Also *Word to the Mother! Word Up* is also the title of a music magazine published in New Jersey. See also WORD IS BORN!

WORD IS BORN!

An affirmative response to a statement or action. Also *Word!, Word up!, Word to the Mother!* A resurfacing of an old, familiar saying in the Black Oral Tradition, "Yo word is yo bond," which was popularized by the FIVE PERCENT NATION in its early years. *Word is born!* reaffirms strong belief in the power of the word, and thus the value of verbal commitment. One's word is the guarantee, the warranty, the *bond,* that whatever was promised will actually occur. *Born* is a result of the AAE pronunciation of "bond"; see Introduction.

WORD TO THE MOTHER!

A response of affirmation. See also WORD IS BORN!, WORD! /WORD UP!

WORK

1) To do something forcefully, completely, with high energy, and persuasively. 2) Used in reference to making something *work* for you with others. "Girlfriend working her pro-

gram," meaning, She is expertly handling some situation or potential conflict. Also *work it.*

WORK A SPOT
To sell drugs or sex in a certain location.

WORK IT
See WORK.

WORK SOMEONE'S NERVES
1) To get on somebody's nerves; to aggravate or irritate a person. 2) To cause emotional stress to a person.

X

1) A reference to Malcolm X, 1960s political theoretician and hero. Born Malcolm Little, he adopted the "X" after he joined the Nation of Islam. 2) Used as the last name of any member of THE NATION. From its inception, THE NATION has followed the practice of substituting an "X" for its members' last names, to symbolize the unknown and lost ancestry of Africans in America and to symbolize rejection of the slavemaster's surname, which was commonly adopted by ex-slaves.

YACUB
According to The NATION, Yacub was a brilliant Black scientist whose curiosity and inventiveness got out of hand and led to the creation of the white man. See also DEVIL.

YAH-YO
> Cocaine.

YELLOW
> See YELLUH.

YELLUH / HIGH YELLUH
> A very light-complexioned African American; praised in some quarters, damned in others. COMMUNITY ambivalence stems from *high yelluhs'* close physical approximation to European Americans. To the extent that white skin is valued, as was the case, for example, in the 1940s and 1950s, then being *yelluh* is a plus. On the other hand, to the extent that a *yelluh* African is a reminder of whiteness/the "enemy," as was the case in the Black Power Movement of the 1960s and 1970s, for instance, then being *yelluh* is a minus. See also COLOR SCALE, COLOR STRUCK, WHOLE LOTTA YELLUH WASTED.

YO!
> 1) A greeting, meaning simply "Hello." 2) Used to get someone's attention, instead of saying "Hey!" or "Hey you!" Possibly from African American military men in the 1950s, who would answer "Yo!" at roll call, whereas their European American counterparts would answer "Yep!"

YO
> "Your," as in "your house," pronounced *yo* following AAE rules; see Introduction. The basketball player who said, "Yo ball" was telling his opponent that it was his turn to get the ball; he was not greeting or talking to the ball, as a confused European American onlooker mistakenly perceived.

YO MOMMA!
> Your mother; a standard formulaic phrase of ritualized insult, from the verbal game of PLAYing THE DOZENS. See the DOZENS.

. . . .

YO THANG
    See DO ONE'S OWN THANG.

YO-YO
    A weak, stupid person.

Z

Z'S
    Sleep. Crossover term.

PERMISSIONS